Who Killed Iago?

Also by James Walton

THE FABER BOOK OF SMOKING

Who Killed Iago?

A Book of Fiendishly
Challenging Literary Quizzes

JAMES WALTON

A PERIGEE BOOK

A PERIGEE BOOK
Published by the Penguin Group
Penguin Group (USA) Inc.
375 Hudson Street, New York, New York 10014, USA
Penguin Group (Canada), 90 Eglinton Avenue East, Suite 700, Toronto, Ontario M4P 2Y3, Canada
(a division of Pearson Penguin Canada Inc.)
Penguin Books Ltd., 80 Strand, London WC2R 0RL, England
Penguin Group Ireland, 25 St. Stephen's Green, Dublin 2, Ireland (a division of Penguin Books Ltd.)
Penguin Group (Australia), 250 Camberwell Road, Camberwell, Victoria 3124, Australia
(a division of Pearson Australia Group Pty. Ltd.)
Penguin Books India Pvt. Ltd., 11 Community Centre, Panchsheel Park, New Delhi—110 017, India
Penguin Group (NZ), 67 Apollo Drive, Rosedale, North Shore 0632, New Zealand
(a division of Pearson New Zealand Ltd.)
Penguin Books (South Africa) (Pty.) Ltd., 24 Sturdee Avenue, Rosebank, Johannesburg 2196,
South Africa

Penguin Books Ltd., Registered Offices: 80 Strand, London WC2R 0RL, England

While the author has made every effort to provide accurate telephone numbers and Internet addresses at the time of publication, neither the publisher nor the author assumes any responsibility for errors, or for changes that occur after publication. Further, the publisher does not have any control over and does not assume any responsibility for author or third-party websites or their content.

WHO KILLED IAGO?

First American edition: June 2009
Originally published as *Sonnets, Bonnets and Bennetts* in Great Britain in 2008 by Faber and Faber Ltd.

Perigee trade paperback ISBN: 978-0-399-53499-7

PRINTED IN THE UNITED STATES OF AMERICA

10 9 8 7 6 5 4 3 2 1

Most Perigee books are available at special quantity discounts for bulk purchases for sales promotions, premiums, fund-raising, or educational use. Special books, or book excerpts, can also be created to fit specific needs. For details, write: Special Markets, Penguin Group (USA) Inc., 375 Hudson Street, New York, New York 10014.

In memory of Ted Walton (1929–2007)
A true quizzer

Introduction

The questions in this book are based on a BBC Radio quiz show called *The Write Stuff*, which I've written for and hosted since 1998. The show features teams of writers battling away—often, as you'd imagine, quite competitively—to display their literary knowledge. It's also allowed me to fulfill a childhood dream. When I was growing up, quizzes figured so prominently at home that, while other boys dreamed of becoming train conductors, firemen, or football players, I hoped that one day I might get to say, "Fingers on the buzzers, please" to people who weren't members of my family—and who actually had buzzers.

Luckily for American readers (and perhaps some British ones, too), there's no need to have heard, or heard of, the program to do the quizzes here. All you need is some literary knowledge of your own, or even just literary interest.

There are ten quizzes, and each quiz has five rounds. The first is what on the show would be called a quick-fire round—where the first person to press his or her buzzer gets the chance to answer. (The questions in each Round One have a linking theme but are otherwise miscellaneous.) It is, of course, entirely up to you whether you do the quick-fire rounds simply to test yourself, or play them with other people in any number of ways. You can ask each player a question in turn. You can read out the questions and see who shouts out the answer first. You can

1

suggest people have imaginary buzzers and ask them to say "buzz" when they think they know the answer. (Or maybe that's just a British thing.)

Next come six extracts to identify, all of which contain solid clues to the book and writer, and, in most cases, are intended to be an entertaining read as well. After that, there's another quick-fire round on a featured author: again, aimed at the general book lover, but with the occasional trickier question slipped in to test that author's true fans.

Round Four is at first sight (and possibly all subsequent ones) the most fiendish—where you have to find the link between four literary people or things. Sometimes the link is factual, in which case the question will usually make that clear. More often, the connecting theme is not itself specifically literary. Either way, the key to success is not to panic. If you calmly take each of the four in turn, you should find one or two that provide the way in, and from there the rest will ideally fall into place—although I admit it's still the hardest round. Every quiz then ends with another quick-fire burst, this time with the theme (except for Quizzes 7 and 10) in the answers rather than the questions.

Meanwhile, as you'll see, there's more to read than in the average quiz book. For the answers, particularly to the non-quick-fire rounds, I've thrown in plenty of extra information that's meant, even for non-quizzers, to be interesting and satisfying in its own right.

And so to the thorny business of awarding points. Needless to say, you're welcome to work out any scoring system you want. (Or, for that matter not to—because I understand there are some otherwise perfectly normal people out there who like to do quizzes "just for fun.") Even so, I thought it might help if I gave some suggestions based on what happens on the show. Correct answers in the quick-fire rounds get one point each. In the extracts round they normally get two: one for the book, another for the author—and where there's any change from that system in the book, I'll explain it as it comes up. In the connections round, I'd suggest a maximum of five: one point for each of the four component parts you identify, and one for getting the link itself.

Finally, to cover myself against the purists: in the extracts, I've sometimes replaced a crucial name with a pronoun—or vice versa to help with identification. I haven't bothered either with ellipses for missing words . . . [or square brackets for words I've moved around slightly] . . . on the grounds . . . that this would be . . . far too . . . distracting. (See what I mean?)

Happy quizzing!

James Walton

Quiz One

Round One

Literary Firsts and One-offs

1. Which literary character's first words to whom are: "How are you? You have been in Afghanistan, I perceive?"

2. Which writer's first names were John Ronald Reuel?

3. Who was the first American writer to win the Nobel Prize for Literature—in 1930, if that helps?

4. Who won the 2008 Pulitzer Prize for fiction with his first novel, *The Brief Wondrous Life of Oscar Wao*?

5. What's the title of Maya Angelou's first volume of autobiography?

6. What's the only book for children by James Bond's creator, Ian Fleming?

7. Who, in 1940, was the first African American author to be chosen for the Book-of-the-Month Club, with his novel *Native Son*?

8. What are the first three words of Herman Melville's *Moby-Dick*?

9. Who wrote the 1984 novel *First Among Equals*?

10. Who, in 1975, became the only fictional character to receive an obituary in the *New York Times*? (Clue: The character's creator was British, but the character wasn't.)

 Answers on p. 21

Round Two

Pedants' Revolt: A Round of Literary Mistakes

In each of the following passages, the author has made some technical or factual error. Can you identify the author, the work—and the mistake in question? (If you should happen to be quizzing seriously, there's one point for the book, one point for the author, and two for the mistake.)

1. "His specs—use them as burning glasses!"
   Piggy was surrounded before he could back away.
   "Here—Let me go!" His voice rose to a shriek of terror as Jack snatched the glasses off his face. "Mind out! Give 'em back! I can hardly see!"
   Ralph moved the lenses back and forth till a glossy white image of the declining sun lay on a piece of rotten wood. Almost at once a thin trickle of smoke rose up. A tiny flame appeared.

2. L—, light of my life, fire of my loins. My sin, my soul. L—: the tip of the tongue taking a trip of three steps down the palate to tap, at three, at the teeth.

3. Cannon to right of them,
   Cannon to left of them,
   Cannon in front of them
       Volley'd and thunder'd;
   Storm'd at with shot and shell,

 Answers on p. 23

Boldly they rode and well,
  Into the jaws of Death,
  Into the mouth of Hell
  Rode the six hundred.

4. Antigonus: Thou art perfect then our ship hath
   touched upon
        The deserts of Bohemia?
   Mariner: Ay, my lord, and fear
   We have landed in ill time; the skies look grimly,
   And threaten present blusters.

5. This one appeared in the first edition only:

Stephen Wraysford's metal trunk had been sent
ahead and was waiting at the foot of the bed. He
unpacked his clothes and hung his spare suit in the
giant carved wardrobe. The room was simple but
had been decorated with some care. There was a
vase of blue peonies on the table and prints of
street scenes in Honfleur on either side of the door.

6. This is from a well-regarded novel of 2007, which
   begins one night in 1962—but here flashes back to
   the summer of 1961, where a rock-and-roll fan is trying to educate his classical-music-loving girlfriend:

He brought to Oxford from the cottage a selection
of records he wanted her to learn to love. She sat
dead still and listened patiently, with closed eyes
and too much concentration, to Chuck Berry. He
thought she might dislike "Roll over Beethoven," but
she found it hilarious. He played her "clumsy but
honourable" cover versions of Chuck Berry songs by

the Beatles and Rolling Stones. She tried to find something appreciative to say about each one, but she used words like "bouncy" or "merry" or "heart-felt," and he knew she was simply being kind.

(Clue: That night in 1962 is a wedding night.)

     Answer on p. 25

Round Three

Featured Author: Jane Austen

1. In which county was Jane Austen born?

2. What did Austen's father do for a living?

3. In *Mansfield Park*, who owns Mansfield Park?

4. In *Pride and Prejudice*, what's Mr. Darcy's first name?

5. Of which novel did Austen write in advance: "I am going to take a heroine whom no one but myself will much like"?

6. What was the name of Jane's confidante and sister?

7. Which novel began as a sketch written by Austen in her early twenties called *Elinor and Marianne*?

8. To which public figure is *Emma* dedicated?

9. What's the fourth word of *Pride and Prejudice*?

10. Within one either way, how many Austen novels were published in her lifetime?

     Answers on p. 27

Round Four

A Round on the Links: Literary Connections

Can you link the following literary people or things?

1. *The Big Sleep*

   Holden Caulfield's sister in *The Catcher in the Rye*

   The founder and first editor of the *New Yorker*

   Daphne du Maurier's eponymous cousin

2. (These come in the correct order.)

   Randle P. McMurphy in a novel of 1962

   The Book of Exodus, Chapter 20 verses 3–17

   The breakthrough novel by the only-ever Colombian winner of the Nobel Prize for Literature

   The breakthrough novel by Jane Smiley

3. Peter, Susan, Edmund, and Lucy are evacuated to the house of an old professor

   Kurt Vonnegut's ice-nine

   William Blake's "fearful symmetry"

   Don Fabrizio, Prince of Salina, in a 1958 novel set in Sicily around one hundred years earlier

Answer on pp. 29–30

4. Johann Wyss

   A John Fowles novel of 1969

   The sonnet sequence that contains the poem beginning: "How do I love thee? Let me count the ways"

   Michael Ondaatje wins the 1992 Booker Prize

Answer on pp. 30–32

Round Five

Literary Festival: A Christmas Round

All the answers here contain, or indeed comprise, a word associated with Christmas.

1. Which country is the setting for Louis de Bernières's novel *Birds Without Wings*—the long-awaited successor to *Corelli's Mandolin*?

2. Who's the main character in Truman Capote's *Breakfast at Tiffany's*?

3. In George Orwell's *Animal Farm*, which character represents Leon Trotsky?

4. Who wrote the controversial 1963 novel *The Group*?

5. Who wrote the 2008 novel *Netherland*?

6. Which Austrian writer and thinker founded the movement known as anthroposophy?

7. Whose novels include *The Stone Diaries* and *Larry's Party*?

8. What was the first novel by Thomas Wolfe?

9. What was the first novel by Pamela Anderson?

10. Which city is the setting for the Ed Eagle novels by Stuart Woods?

    Answers on p. 33

Quiz One: Answers

Round One

Literary Firsts and One-offs

1. Sherlock Holmes to Dr. Watson in *A Study in Scarlet* (1887). Holmes, as it turns out, is right about Afghanistan.

2. J. R. R. Tolkien

3. Sinclair Lewis

4. Junot Díaz

5. *I Know Why the Caged Bird Sings*

6. *Chitty Chitty Bang Bang*

7. Richard Wright. The second was Toni Morrison with *Song of Solomon*, thirty-seven years later.

8. "Call me Ishmael."

9. Jeffrey Archer

10. Hercule Poirot—following his death in *Curtain*, a book Agatha Christie wrote in the 1940s to be Poirot's last case when the time came. She eventually published it the year before her own death, realizing by then that she couldn't write any more original novels.

Round Two

Pedants' Revolt: A Round of Literary Mistakes

1. From *The Lord of the Flies* by William Golding. The mistake, now something of a classic, is (as all well-read opticians will know) that Piggy is short-sighted—and so the lenses of his specs would have diverged rather than concentrated the sun's rays. As a result, they could not have been used to start a fire.

2. The celebrated opening lines of *Lolita* by Vladimir Nabokov, where Humbert Humbert is explaining the phonetics of his beloved's name: Lo. Lee. Ta. Oddly, though, despite being no mean pedants themselves, Nabokov and Humbert have got it wrong. As the *Times Literary Supplement* quickly pointed out at the time, neither in English nor in Russian does a "t" sound tap at the teeth. It is, phonetically speaking, alveolar, which means the tongue strikes the gums where the roots of the upper teeth lie. Not only that, but surely the tongue doesn't take a trip of three steps down the palate either—from Lo to Lee it actually moves upward. Do try this at home.

3. From "The Charge of the Light Brigade" by Alfred, Lord Tennyson. In fact, as Tennyson discovered after he'd sent off the poem for publication, the number of riders going half a league onward that fateful day was nearer seven hundred than six. Even

so, he was unrepentant. "Six," he said, "is much better than seven hundred metrically, so keep it."

4. From *The Winter's Tale* where Shakespeare gives landlocked Bohemia a coastline. Ever since Ben Jonson ridiculed this howler in 1619, critics have tried hard to explain it away: saying it's a deliberate sign to the audience that the play is taking place in a magical world, that Bohemia was a misprint for Bithynia, and so on. A more obvious theory— that Shakespeare didn't care much one way or the other—has maybe never been taken seriously enough.

5. From the first edition of *Birdsong* by Sebastian Faulks—and the mistake is a botanical one. Peonies can only be crimson or white, not blue. In later editions, "blue peonies" was replaced with the cunningly vague "wild flowers."

6. From Ian McEwan's *On Chesil Beach*, based around a disastrous wedding night in 1962. Yet, in those happier days of their courtship, Edward couldn't have played Florence records by the Beatles or the Rolling Stones. By that stage of the summer of 1961, the Beatles hadn't released any, didn't get a British recording deal until 1962—and, wouldn't record a Chuck Berry cover until "Roll over Beethoven" in late 1963. The Stones, meanwhile, didn't play their first gig until July 1962. No wonder that in the paperback edition of the novel, the Beatles and Stones have mysteriously disappeared and Edward just plays Chuck Berry. Nonetheless, this seems a curious mistake for McEwan to have made, given that *On Chesil*

Beach is set so carefully in the time that Philip Larkin described as being before "sexual intercourse began / In nineteen sixty-three / Between the end of the *Chatterley* ban / And the Beatles' first LP."

Round Three

Featured Author: Jane Austen

1. Hampshire

2. He was a clergyman (in Steventon, Hampshire; Jane was born in the rectory)

3. Sir Thomas Bertram

4. Fitzwilliam

5. *Emma*

6. Cassandra

7. *Sense and Sensibility*, in which the two main characters are still called Elinor and Marianne

8. The Prince Regent. In Austen's defense, it was a dedication she was more or less bullied into and very reluctantly made.

9. "Truth"—as in "It is a truth universally acknowledged, that a single man in possession of a good fortune must be in want of a wife."

10. Four: *Sense and Sensibility*, *Pride and Prejudice*, *Emma*, and *Mansfield Park*. *Persuasion* and *Northanger Abbey* were both published the year after her death at the age of forty-one. (Various unfinished works and books she wrote as a girl have followed since, but those are still the big six.)

Round Four

A Round on the Links: Literary Connections

1. CHARACTERS ON *FRIENDS*

   The Big Sleep was the first novel by Raymond <u>Chandler</u>.

   <u>Phoebe</u> is Holden's much-loved little sister in J. D. Salinger's novel, and about the only person he regards as not a phony.

   After founding the *New Yorker*, Harold <u>Ross</u> edited all 1,399 issues from the first until his death in 1951—the same year, coincidentally, that Daphne du Maurier published *My Cousin <u>Rachel</u>*.

2. NUMBERS THAT ARE TEN TIMES THE PREVIOUS ONE (OR, IF YOU PREFER, THE BASE TEN NUMERAL SYSTEM)

   Randle P. McMurphy is the main character of Ken Kesey's *<u>One</u> Flew over the Cuckoo's Nest*.

   Those verses from Exodus contain the <u>Ten</u> Commandments.

   The breakthrough book by Colombia's Gabriel García Márquez was *<u>One Hundred</u> Years of Solitude*, which came out in 1967, fifteen years before he was awarded the Nobel Prize. The novel is generally credited with introducing the world to magic realism.

Jane Smiley won the 1992 Pulitzer Prize for _A Thousand Acres_, which transferred the characters and themes of _King Lear_ to a farm in 1980s Iowa.

3. CATS, BIG AND SMALL

It's in the professor's house that Peter, Susan, and the rest soon discover the <u>lion</u>, the witch, and the wardrobe—not necessarily in that order—in C. S. Lewis's novel.

In Vonnegut's _Cat's Cradle_, ice-nine is a substance that can turn all water on Earth to ice. When, in his "autobiographical collage" _Palm Sunday_, Vonnegut gave grades to all his works, _Cat's Cradle_ was one of only two to get an A-plus, along with _Slaughterhouse-Five_. (_Palm Sunday_ itself got only a C, but still did better than _Slapstick_ and _Happy Birthday, Wanda June_—both of which got Ds.) On the whole, critics have not tended to disagree with Vonnegut's own assessments.

"Fearful symmetry" is a phrase from Blake's poem _The <u>Tyger</u>_—the one that begins "Tyger! Tyger! burning bright,/ In the forests of the night."

Don Fabrizio is better known as the <u>Leopard</u> in the posthumously published novel of that name by Giuseppe Tomasi di Lampedusa, about a Sicilian nobleman during the unification of Italy.

4. EUROPEAN-COUNTRY-RELATED ADJECTIVES

Johann Wyss, a pastor by trade, became one of literature's great one-hit wonders in 1812 when he wrote *The Swiss Family Robinson*. His tale of a family shipwrecked on an island was primarily designed to teach children the importance of Christian values. It was also much influenced by *Robinson Crusoe*—hence the title.

Fowles's 1969 novel was *The French Lieutenant's Woman*, an affectionate parody of a Victorian novel, although one with three different endings to the main love story.

Elizabeth Barrett Browning told the story of her love for Robert Browning in *Sonnets from the Portuguese*—which contained "How Do I Love Thee?" The title of the sequence was chosen partly to disguise how personal the poems were, by suggesting that they were a translation. But there was an in-joke there, too: "the Portuguese" was Robert's nickname for Elizabeth, because of her dark complexion. The Brownings were forced to marry in secret—because her tyrannical father forbade any of his adult children to marry anyone ever. (Elizabeth was forty at the time.) They then eloped to Italy, where they spent most of their time until her death in 1861. Throughout that time, too, she was generally considered a better poet than he was.

In 1992 the second dead heat in Booker Prize history saw *Sacred Hunger* by Barry Unsworth sharing the award with Michael Ondaatje's *English Patient*, which went on to achieve another historic second—as a Booker winner that became a film that went on to win the Oscar for Best Picture. The only previous example was *Schindler's Ark* by Thomas Keneally, filmed by Steven Spielberg under its American title of *Schindler's List*.

Round Five

Literary Festival: A Christmas Round

1. Turkey
2. <u>Holly</u> Golightly
3. Snowball
4. <u>Mary</u> McCarthy
5. <u>Joseph</u> O'Neill
6. <u>Rudolf</u> Steiner
7. <u>Carol</u> Shields
8. *Look Homeward, <u>Angel</u>*
9. *Star*
10. <u>Santa</u> Fe

Quiz Two

Round One

Literary Twosomes, Couples, and Double Acts

1. Which two German academics gave Disney the plots for *Cinderella*, *Snow White and the Seven Dwarfs*, and *Sleeping Beauty*?

2. The New York cousins, Frederic Dannay and Manfred B. Lee, created which fictional detective—whose name they also used as their joint pseudonym?

3. Who wrote the 1965 play *The Odd Couple*?

4. As whom are Proteus and Valentine better known in a play of the 1590s?

5. Whose crime novels include *Knots & Crosses*, *Black & Blue*, and *Hide & Seek*?

6. Which same two emotions feature in the titles of two books published by Hunter S. Thompson in 1972 and 1973?

7. Which couple provide the title for a 1988 novel by Peter Carey?

8. Who were the parents of Mary Shelley, the author of *Frankenstein*?

9. Which two poets published *Lyrical Ballads* in 1798?

10. Whose first novel, in 1939, was called *At Swim-Two-Birds*?

     Answers on p. 51

Round Two

Carry On Reading: Double Entendre in Classic Literature

For the following passages, please identify the book and author responsible for these unintentional moments of what some purists might consider to be cheap comedy. In all cases, the proper nouns should be a clue.

1. A kindly bachelor, and organist, falls in love in a novel of 1844:

   It must be acknowledged that, asleep or awake, Tom's position in reference to this young lady was full of uneasiness. The more he saw of her, the more he admired her beauty, her intelligence, the amiable qualities that even won on the divided house of Pecksniff, and in a few days restored at all events the semblance of harmony and kindness between the two angry sisters. When she spoke, Tom held his breath, so eagerly he listened; when she sang, he sat like one entranced. She touched his organ, and from that bright epoch, even it, the old companion of his happiest hours, incapable as he had thought of elevation, began a new and deified existence.

2. From a chapter called "Enter the Aunts and Uncles" in a novel of 1860:

   The Dodsons were certainly a handsome family, and Mrs. Glegg was not the least handsome of the sisters. As she sat in Mrs. Tulliver's arm-chair, no impartial observer could have denied that for a woman of fifty she had a very comely face and figure, though Tom and Maggie considered their aunt Glegg as the type of ugliness. It is true she despised the advantages of costume, for though, as she often observed, no woman had better clothes, it was not her way to wear her new things out before her old ones. Mrs. Glegg had doubtless the glossiest and crispest brown curls in her drawers, as well as curls in various degrees of fuzzy laxness.

3. From a novel of 1847:

This lane inclined uphill all the way to Hay; having reached the middle, I sat down on a stile which led thence into a field. Gathering my mantle about me, and sheltering my hands in my muff, I did not feel the cold, though it froze keenly; as was attested by a sheet of ice covering the causeway, where a little brooklet, now congealed, had overflowed after a rapid thaw some days since. From my seat I could look down on Thornfield: the grey and battle-mented hall was the principal object in the vale below me.

4. From a novel of 1816:

Mrs. Goddard was the mistress of a School—not of a seminary, or an establishment, or any thing which professed, in long sentences of refined nonsense, to combine liberal acquirements with elegant morality upon new principles and new systems—and where young ladies for enormous pay might be screwed out of health and into vanity—but a real, honest, old-fashioned Boarding-school.

(Clue: One of the pupils at Mrs. Goddard's school
is called Harriet Smith.)

5. The lovers get together at last—in a literary heavy-weight's second novel in 1872, whose title is a quotation from Shakespeare's *As You Like It*:

    Here, upon the bright after-glow about the horizon, was now visible an irregular shape, which at first he conceived to be a bough standing a little beyond the line of its neighbours. Then it seemed to move, and, as he advanced still further, there was no doubt that it was a living being sitting in the bank, head bowed on hand. The grassy margin entirely prevented his footsteps from being heard, and it was not till he was close that the figure recognised him. Up it sprang, and he was face to face with Fancy.
    "Dick, Dick! O, is it you, Dick!"
    "Yes, Fancy," said Dick in a rather repentant tone, and lowering his nuts.

6. Finally in this round, another early novel by a literary heavyweight, this one from 1876—and here you even get the first name of the eponymous hero. (He's the one with the beautiful soul.)

    Roderick sat staring a moment longer at the floor, then he sprang up and laid his hand affectionately on his friend's shoulder. "You are the best man in the world," he said, "and I am a vile brute. Only," he added in a moment, "you don't understand me!" And

Answers on pp. 53–54

he looked at him with eyes of such radiant lucidity that one might have said (and Rowland did almost say so, himself) that it was the fault of one's own grossness if one failed to read to the bottom of that beautiful soul.

Rowland smiled sadly. "What is it now? Explain."

"Oh, I can't explain!" cried Roderick impatiently, returning to his work. "I have only one way of expressing my deepest feelings—it's this!" And he swung his tool.

Answer on p. 54

Round Three

Featured Author: Stephen King

1. In King's first novel *Carrie*, what's Carrie's surname?

2. Despite the success of the book and the film, in what way was *Carrie* a huge flop in 1988?

3. Which King novel features Annie Wilkes, a psychotic nurse?

4. Which King novel consists entirely of a monologue from a sixty-five-year-old cleaning woman?

5. Which film star appears in the title of the King novella on which the movie *The Shawshank Redemption* is based?

6. Under what name did King publish some of his early novels, including *Thinner* and *The Running Man*?

7. Which thousand-page King novel has a one-word, two-letter title?

8. In June 1999, what impact did Bryan Smith have on King's life?

9. According to King, during his drinking years, which novel about a rabid St. Bernard dog did he have almost no memory of writing?

10. In *The Shining*, what's the name of the main character—a recovering alcoholic writer?

Answers on p. 55

Round Four

A Round on the Links: Literary Connections

Can you link the following literary people or things?

1. *Ma Rainey's Black Bottom*

    The Sportswriter

    Up from Slavery: An Autobiography

    The 1755 Dictionary of the English Language (twice)

2. In 1985 Oliver Sacks has one of the few bestsellers in literary history about neurology

    John le Carré's tailor

    The Scottish farmer whose horse loses her tail to a witch in a poem by Robert Burns

    What seems from all available statistics to have been the bestselling novel of the nineteenth century

3. What seems from all available statistics (although perhaps more reliable ones this time) to have been the bestselling novel of the 1970s

    Bertholt Brecht's 1939 play set during the Thirty Years' War

    Barbara Trapido's first novel

    Theodore Dreiser's first novel

Answers on pp. 57–59

4. (A children's book special:)

   T. H. White's sequence of Arthurian novels

   The Hans Christian Andersen story in which Gerda rescues Kay

   Antoine de Saint-Exupéry's only book for children

   Meg Cabot

Round Five

One After the Other: An Alphabetical Round

Q2

All the answers here consist of two words, which in each case begin with consecutive letters of the alphabet.

1. What's the third in Louisa M. Alcott's series of novels about the March sisters?

2. What's the actual name (i.e., not the nickname) of the most famous literary creation of Leslie Charteris?

3. Which literary novelist gave the eulogy at the memorial service for Benny Hill?

4. Which thousand-page novel of 1996 is set in a North America where Canada, the United States, and Mexico are unified?

5. Whose last two novels were *The Years* and *Between the Acts*?

6. Whose first book was *A Heartbreaking Work of Staggering Genius*?

7. *Frederica, Venetia*, and *The Black Sheep* are among whose Regency romances—a genre she's generally credited with inventing?

8. Whose plays include *The Wild Duck* and *Hedda Gabler*?

     Answers on p. 61

9. What two words are missing from the title of this poem by Wallace Stevens: "— — at the Clavier"?

10. Who, by the time of her death in 2000, had apparently written 723 novels?

Answers on p. 61

Quiz Two: Answers

Round One

Literary Twosomes, Couples, and Double Acts

1. The Brothers Grimm (Jakob and Wilhelm), nineteenth-century medieval historians, comparative linguists, and, on the side, collectors of fairy tales

2. Ellery Queen

3. Neil Simon

4. The Two Gentlemen of Verona, in Shakespeare's play

5. Ian Rankin

6. Fear and loathing—with the novel *Fear and Loathing in Las Vegas* and the journalism collection *Fear and Loathing: On the Campaign Trail '72*

7. Oscar and Lucinda

8. William Godwin and Mary Wollstonecraft—respectively, the radical philosopher and the author of *A Vindication of the Rights of Woman.* Wollstonecraft died of a fever ten days after Mary's birth.

9. William Wordsworth and Samuel Taylor Coleridge

10. Flann O'Brien

Round Two

Carry On Reading: Double Entendre in Classic Literature

1. From *Martin Chuzzlewit* by Charles Dickens. Tom Pinch is the trusting assistant of the hypocritical Mr. Pecksniff, and the woman touching his organ is Mary Graham, Martin's fiancée. Still, at least Martin proves sympathetic to his friend's plight. He promises that when he and Mary are married, they'll build Tom a music room to play his organ in: "There you shall play away, Tom, till you tire yourself; and, as you like to do so in the dark, it shall *be* dark; and many's the summer evening Mary and I will sit and listen to you, Tom; be sure of that!"

2. From *The Mill on the Floss* by George Eliot. Eliot is, naturally, referring to Mrs. Glegg's habit of not wearing the wigs she kept at home in drawers.

3. From *Jane Eyre* by Charlotte Brontë, with Jane taking a walk from Thornfield Hall where she's become the governess to Mr. Rochester's ward, Adèle Varens. At this stage, she still hasn't met the man himself, but it's while on this walk that she meets a handsome stranger whose horse slips on the ice—and who duly turns out to be Mr. Rochester.

4. From Jane Austen's *Emma*—where Mrs. Goddard's pupil Harriet Smith will later become Emma's pet project.

5. From Thomas Hardy's *Under the Greenwood Tree*—with Dick Dewy and Fancy Day finally about to overcome their many misunderstandings. Dick of course had just been out collecting nuts, or as Hardy puts it: "Never man nutted as Dick nutted that afternoon."

6. From *Roderick Hudson* by Henry James, the story of a young Massachusetts sculptor and a profoundly serious exploration of the nature of art.

Round Three

Featured Author: Stephen King

1. White

2. As a Broadway musical. It opened on May 12 and closed on May 15.

3. *Misery*

4. *Dolores Claiborne*

5. Rita Hayworth—the novella's title being *Rita Hayworth and Shawshank Redemption*

6. Richard Bachman. (At the time, his publishers didn't think he should be bringing out more than one book a year under his own name.)

7. *It*

8. Smith was driving the van that knocked King down, leaving him with a shattered right leg, a chipped spine, and a lacerated skull

9. *Cujo*

10. Jack Torrance—played in the film of course by Jack Nicholson, whose performance King apparently considered a bit over the top

Round Four

A Round on the Links: Literary Connections

1. THE SAME SURNAMES AS AMERICAN PRESIDENTS

Ma Rainey's Black Bottom was one of the ten plays in "The Pittsburgh Cycle" by August <u>Wilson</u>— although the only one not set in Pittsburgh. Each play focuses on a different decade of the twentieth century, with *Ma Rainey* the first to be written, set in Chicago in the 1920s.

The Sportswriter by Richard <u>Ford</u> also turned out to be the first in a sequence. After its success in 1986, two further Ford novels, *Independence Day* and *The Lay of the Land*, followed the main character, Frank Bascombe, through his largely unhappy life.

Up from Slavery was the 1901 autobiography of Booker T. <u>Washington</u>. It made such an immediate impact that later the same year Washington became the first African American to be invited to the White House, by Theodore Roosevelt.

The dictionary produced in just nine years by Dr. Samuel <u>Johnson</u> (as in Andrew *and* Lyndon B.— hence "twice") remained without a serious rival in Britain until the *Oxford English Dictionary*, which took fifty years to compile and was completed in 1928. Johnson's definitions famously reflect his own prejudices, especially his anti-Scottish ones. ("Oats: a grain which in England is generally given to horses, but in Scotland supports the people.") The word "lexicographer" he defined as "A writer of dictionaries, a harmless drudge."

2. HATS

Oliver Sacks is the neurologist whose bestselling collections of case studies include 1985's *Man who Mistook His Wife for a <u>Hat</u>*. (His other big hit was *Awakenings*, which became a movie starring Robert de Niro and Robin Williams.)

John le Carré wrote *The Tailor of <u>Panama</u>*.

The Scottish farmer was <u>Tam o'Shanter</u> in the poem by Burns, which influenced the language in more ways than that one. Not only did the Tam o'Shanter hat get its name from the protagonist, but a famous ship was also named after the witch's shirt in the poem: a cutty sark.

The bestselling novel of the nineteenth century (and presumably of all time until then) is generally thought to have been *<u>Trilby</u>* by George du Maurier, Daphne's grandfather. Published in 1894, his tale of how the eponymous artist's model becomes a singing star remained a sensation for many years. Although it's not read so much these days, several of its phrases are, like those of "Tam o'Shanter," still around. The trilby itself got its name from the type of headgear the heroine wore in Beerbohm Tree's stage version; her mysterious mentor is called Svengali; and her preferred euphemism for posing nude is "in the altogether." *Trilby* was such a huge

hit in America, too, that a town in Florida was
named after it.

3. MEMBERS OF A NUCLEAR FAMILY

The bestselling novel of the 1970s was *The Godfather* by Mario Puzo, actually published in 1969, but a bestseller for years thanks, not least, to the Godfather films.

Brecht's 1939 play was *Mother Courage and her Children*.

Barbara Trapido's first novel was *Brother of the More Famous Jack* in 1982.

Theodore Dreiser's first novel was *Sister Carrie* (1900)—which has followed more or less the opposite path from the previous question's *Trilby*: considered a classic now, it made almost no impact when it first came out. Because of its amoral and, worse still, unpunished heroine, Dreiser's publishers insisted on several cuts and even after that, still refused to promote it. His original version wasn't published until 1981.

4. MEMBERS OF A NUCLEAR ROYAL FAMILY

In 1958, T. H. White collected his four novels about King Arthur into the book, *The Once and Future King*. The first novel in the sequence was *The Sword in the Stone*, and the last was *The Candle in the Wind*, a title later borrowed, as you may have noticed, by Elton John.

The Hans Christian Andersen story is "The Snow Queen."

Saint-Exupéry's *Little Prince* (1943), despite being narrated by an airman stranded in the desert, is also one of his few books not primarily about flying—because Saint-Exupéry was a pioneering pilot as well as a writer. He disappeared in 1944, while on a reconnaissance mission to spy on German troop movements. The discovery of his plane's wreckage, in 2000, was a major news story in France, where the international airport in his home town is now called Lyon-Saint-Exupéry—and where, before the euro was introduced, he and his own drawing of the little prince featured on the fifty-franc note.

Meg Cabot's highly successful series of books for girls is the Princess Diaries, the first volume of which appeared in 2000.

Round Five

One After the Other: An Alphabetical Round

1. *Little Men*—the first two being *Little Women* and *Good Wives* (now often published together)

2. Simon Templar—aka The Saint

3. Anthony Burgess. Burgess believed that Hill's comedy was a masterly study of male sexual regret, and in the eulogy compared him to, among others, Plautus, Falstaff, and Rabelais.

4. *Infinite Jest* by David Foster Wallace

5. Virginia Woolf

6. Dave Eggers

7. Georgette Heyer

8. Henrik Ibsen

9. Peter Quince

10. Barbara Cartland, who in her heyday was producing a book a fortnight

Quiz Three

Round One

World of Books: Literary Globetrotting

1. Which novel opens with Raskolnikov walking out into the streets of St. Petersburg?

2. Which literary hero lives in St. Petersburg with his Aunt Polly and his half brother Sid?

3. In which 1990s novel does Quoyle rebuild his life in Newfoundland?

4. In which language did Franz Kafka write?

5. Who, in the 1850s, wrote the highly influential three-volume work of art history *The Stones of Venice*?

6. Who, in the 1950s, wrote the highly influential food books *French Country Cooking* and *Italian Food*?

7. What's the main title of the Bill Bryson book that's subtitled *Travels in Europe*?

8. Which country is the setting for *Things Fall Apart* by Chinua Achebe?

9. Who wrote the 2000 romantic novel *Zabibah and the King*—which received rave reviews in all of the newspapers in Iraq, became a bestseller there, and won the Baghdad Book Club Award?

10. Which African American writer died in Ghana, as a Ghanian citizen, the day before Martin Luther King Jr. delivered his "I have a dream" speech?

Answers on p. 79

Round Two

Fact and Fiction

All of the following passages feature real-life people turning up in novels. Please identify the book and author in each case.

1. A passage set in the 1970s, but from a twenty-first-century bestseller. (Baba in this context means father.)

   We saw our first Western together, *Rio Bravo* with John Wayne, at the Cinema Park, across the street from my favorite bookstore. I remember begging Baba to take us to Iran so we could meet John Wayne. Baba burst out in gales of his deep-throated laughter and, when he could talk again, explained to us the concept of voice dubbing. Hassan and I were stunned. Dazed. John Wayne didn't really speak Farsi and he wasn't Iranian! He was American, just like the friendly, longhaired men and women we always saw hanging around in Kabul, dressed in their tattered, brightly colored shirts. We saw *Rio Bravo* three times, but we saw our favorite Western, *The Magnificent Seven*, thirteen times. With each viewing, we cried at the end when the Mexican kids buried Charles Bronson—who, as it turned out, wasn't Iranian either.

2. More movie-going in the next one, where the main character's name has been snipped out—but where

the typography, as well as the content, of his speech should help.

In the spring of '57 —— was especially destructive to the helpless swamplife of Gravesend, and to Mary Magdalene; just before Easter, we'd been to The Idaho, where we suffered through Cecil B. DeMille's *Ten Commandments*–the life of Moses, represented by Charlton Heston undergoing various costume changes and radical hairstyles.

"IT'S ANOTHER MALE-NIPPLE MOVIE," —— said; and, indeed, in addition to Charlton Heston's nipples, there is evidence of Yul Brynner and John Derek and even Edward G. Robinson having nipples, too.

That The Idaho should show *The Ten Commandments* so close to Easter was another example of what my grandmother called the poor "seasonal" taste of nearly everyone in the entertainment business–"ALL THAT OLD-TESTAMENT HARSHNESS WHEN WE SHOULD BE THINKING ABOUT JESUS!" as —— put it. The parting of the Red Sea especially offended him.

3. I hung around for a while feeling a total git, then spotted Simon from Marketing. When I was almost there, however, I noticed that, unfortunately, Simon from Marketing was talking to Julian Barnes. I hovered indecisively then started to sidle away, at which point Simon said in an irritated superior voice (one you, funnily enough, never hear him use when he is trying to get off with you by the photocopier), "Did you want something?"

"Ah! Yes!" I said, panicking wildly about what it

was I could possibly want. Simon and Julian Barnes looked at me expectantly.

"Do you know where the toilets are?" I blurted. Damn. Damn. Why? Why did I say that? I saw a faint smile hover over the thin-but-attractive lips of Julian Barnes.

4. They got a taxi back to Fiona's place. The cabbe was listening to GLR, and the disc jockey was talking about Kurt Cobain; it took Will a while to understand the strange, muted tone in the DJ's voice.

"What's happened to him?" Will asked the cabbie.

"Who?"

"Kurt Cobain."

"Is he the Nirvana geezer? He shot himself in the head. Boom."

"Dead?"

"No. Just a headache. Yeah, course he's dead."

Will wasn't surprised, particularly, and he was too old to be shocked. He hadn't been shocked by the death of a pop star since Marvin Gaye died. He had been . . . how old? The first of April 1984 . . . Jesus, ten years ago. So he had been twenty-six, and still of an age when things like that meant something.

"Isn't he the singer Marcus liked?" Fiona asked him.

5. "Great stuff, the Escapist," Orson Welles told Sammy. He seemed vastly tall and surprisingly young, and he smelled like Dolores Del Rio. In 1941 it was fashionable among certain smart people to confess to a more than passing knowledge of

69   Answers on pp. 81–82

Batman, or Captain Marvel, or the Blue Beetle. "I don't like to miss a word."

"Thank you," said Sam.

This, though he never forgot and in later years embellished it, was the extent of his interaction with Orson Welles, on that night or any other.

6. Finally in this round, the breakthrough novel from 1953 by a future American winner of the Nobel Prize for Literature. The protagonist is hanging round in a Mexican town square when he spots the real-life character—but the final place name mentioned here might be a bigger clue.

The principal figure came out of the center limousine with a spring; he was very gingery and energetic, debonair, sharp, acute in the beard. He addressed himself without waste of attention to the study of the front of the cathedral. As I looked at him I decided with a real jolt that this must be Trotsky, down from Mexico City, the great Russian exile, and my eyes grew big. Head thrown back, Trotsky regarded and estimated the vast church, and with a jump in which hardly anything elderly appeared he went up the stairs and hastened in. There was a surge after him; the people with briefcases—members of the radical organizations I used to know in Chicago always had briefcases like those—went through the dark gap of the church door.

I was excited by this famous figure, and I believe what it was that stirred me up was the instant impression he gave of navigation by the great stars, of being fit to speak the most important human words and universal terms.

Round Three

Featured Author: Thomas Hardy

1. What was Hardy's first profession?

2. As what is Michael Henchard known in the title of a Hardy novel?

3. Which Hardy novel takes its title from a phrase in Thomas Gray's "Elegy Written in a Country Church-Yard"?

4. In *Tess of the d'Urbervilles*, where is Tess arrested for the murder of Alec d'Urberville?

5. Which Hardy novel opens on a Saturday in November, with twilight falling over Egdon Heath?

6. How many times was Hardy married?

7. The savage critical reception of which book is generally agreed to be the reason Hardy gave up writing novels?

8. In *Jude the Obscure*, who hangs Jude and Sue's two youngest children?

9. In his later years, what was the geographically significant name of Hardy's dog?

10. What's unusual about Hardy's final resting place?

 Answers on pp. 83–84

Round Four

A Round on the Links: Literary Connections

Can you link the following literary people or things?

Q3

1. The Edgar Allan Poe story that ends with the unnamed narrator confessing to the murder of an old man

    The first novel by Amy Tan

    The missing word from the title of a short story by F. Scott Fitzgerald: "The — as Big as the Ritz"

    The missing word from the first line of a much-mocked poem by William Wordsworth: "—! with which Wilkinson hath tilled his lands"

2. Vikram Seth's first novel

    Thornton Wilder's 1927 bestseller, set in Peru

    Pierre Boulle's 1952 bestseller, set in Burma

    The love between Robert Kincaid and Francesca Johnson

3. The 1960 novel narrated by Jean Louise Finch

    Beau Geste

    "Hail to thee, blithe Spirit"

    Iain Banks's 1992 road

     Answers on pp. 85–87

4. (A sadly factual one:)

   The Rainbow

   All Quiet on the Western Front

   The Satanic Verses

   Thomas Carlyle's *French Revolution*
   (accidentally)

Answer on p. 87

Round Five

No First Names Here: An Initials Round

All the answers here are people with two initials instead of a first name—and just to make it easier, over the course of the round, the initials come in alphabetical order . . .

Q3

1. Who wrote the poem beginning "Jonathan Jo Has a mouth like an 'O'"?

2. Who wrote the 1981 novel *The White Hotel*?

3. Which American poet wrote the prose work *The Enormous Room*?

4. Who was known as "The Sage of Baltimore"?

5. Which cult horror author wrote *At the Mountains of Madness*?

6. Which writer invented the girl's name "Wendy"?

7. Who created the police detective Adam Dalgliesh?

8. Which private detective first appeared in the 1982 novel *Indemnity Only*?

9. Sylvia Plath killed herself in a house once lived in by which poet?

10. Which poet received a big posthumous boost to his sales from the film *Four Weddings and a Funeral*?

 Answers on p. 89

Quiz Three: Answers

Round One

World of Books: Literary Globetrotting

1. *Crime and Punishment* by Fyodor Dostoevsky

2. Tom Sawyer—in the books by Mark Twain. (In a mildly cunning twist, this particular St. Petersburg is in Missouri.)

3. *The Shipping News* by E. Annie Proulx

4. German—although he was from Prague, his family was German-speaking

5. John Ruskin

6. Elizabeth David

7. *Neither Here Nor There*

8. Nigeria

9. Saddam Hussein. One Iraqi reviewer hailed it as "an innovation in the history of novels" and it later became both a twenty-part television series and a musical.

10. W.E.B. Du Bois

Round Two

Fact and Fiction

1. From *The Kite Runner* by Khaled Hosseini—who, like his narrator Amir, was originally from Afghanistan before settling in the United States in his teens. That scene, as you read, was set in the happy days of the early 1970s when Kabul was best known to Americans as part of the hippie trail.

2. From John Irving's *Prayer for Owen Meaney*. Throughout the novel, Irving represents Owen's "wrecked voice" by putting his dialogue in capital letters. We also know from the opening sentence that the narrator, John Wheelwright—Owen's old boyhood friend from Gravesend, New Hampshire—is "a Christian because of Owen Meaney." (John Wheelwright, incidentally, was also the name of the man who founded Exeter, New Hampshire, on which Gravesend is based.)

3. From *Bridget Jones's Diary* by Helen Fielding, featuring Bridget at a literary party for the launch of *Kafka's Motorbike*. Barnes did appear as a party guest in the film version, but for that incident was replaced by Salman Rushdie, who was felt to be more recognizable to a movie audience. (To his credit, Barnes apparently took the decision pretty well.)

4. From *About a Boy* by Nick Hornby—where Kurt Cobain becomes one of the key shared interests

A3

between cool bachelor Will and Fiona's deeply uncool twelve-year-old son Marcus. The novel's title is based on the Nirvana song "About a Girl."

5. From *The Amazing Ad entures of Kavalier & Clay* by Michael Chabon. Joe Kavalier and Sammy Clay are two comic book artists during the Golden Age of the American comic, and the creators of the Escapist—who, following the success of the novel, was turned into a superhero in a real-life comic book. That scene takes place at the New York premiere of *Citizen Kane*.

6. From Saul Bellow's *Adventures of Augie March*— which opens with the celebrated words, "I am an American, Chicago born." Although in later life, Bellow was regarded, and sometimes pilloried, as a conservative, he'd been a Trotskyist in his youth. (Like Trotsky, Bellow was from a Jewish-Russian family.) In one of the twentieth-century's great near misses, Bellow was in Mexico in 1940 and arranged a meeting with his hero—but on the morning of their appointment Trotsky was assassinated by an agent of Stalin's. "A door into a small side room was opened for us," Bellow wrote later, "and there we saw him. He had just died. A cone of bloody bandages was on his head. His cheeks, his nose, his beard, his throat, were streaked with blood . . ."

Round Three

Featured Author: Thomas Hardy

1. He was an architect. (Max Gate, the large Dorset house in which he lived from 1887 onward, was designed by Hardy himself.)

2. The Mayor of Casterbridge

3. *Far from the Madding Crowd*, Hardy's fourth novel—and the first one successful enough to allow him to take up writing full-time. (The full lines in Gray are: "Far from the madding crowd's ignoble strife,/ Their sober wishes never learned to stray.")

4. At Stonehenge

5. *The Return of the Native*. That opening also features in the Monty Python sketch "Novel Writing from Dorset."("Hello, and welcome to Dorchester, where a very good crowd has turned out to watch local boy Thomas Hardy write his new novel . . .")

6. Twice. His first wife, Emma, died in 1912. His second, Florence, was thirty-nine years his junior.

7. *Jude the Obscure*—or, as it was hilariously dubbed by journalists at the time, *Jude the Obscene*. For the last thirty-three years of his life Hardy wrote only poetry.

8. Jude's son—called Jude, but known as "Old Father Time"—from his relationship with Arabella Donn. In characteristic Hardy fashion, the boy then hangs

himself, too, leaving a note containing the explanation: "Done because we are too menny."

9. Wessex—as in the semi-fictional version of the West Country, where many of his novels are set.

10. There are two of them. His heart was buried in Stinsford, Dorset. The rest of him is in Westminster Abbey—where his pallbearers included John Galsworthy, J. M. Barrie, A. E. Housman, Rudyard Kipling, George Bernard Shaw, Prime Minister Stanley Baldwin, and the leader of the opposition, Ramsay MacDonald.

Round Four

A Round on the Links: Literary Connections

1. SUITS OF CARDS

It's in Poe's *Tell-Tale <u>Heart</u>* that the narrator gives that climactic confession to the police, after he continues to hear his dismembered victim's heart beating underneath the floorboards where he's buried.

Amy Tan's first novel was *The Joy Luck <u>Club</u>*, based on her own experiences as the Californian daughter of Chinese parents.

The Fitzgerald short story is "The <u>Diamond</u> as Big as the Ritz."

The Wordsworth poem begins: "<u>Spade!</u> with which Wilkinson hath tilled his lands"—and really is called "To the Spade of a Friend." It duly shows up in many of those anthologies of bad poems by respected poets.

2. BRIDGES

Vikram Seth's second novel, *A Suitable Boy* (1993), is one of the longest ever published, at nearly 600,000 words. His first, *<u>The Golden Gate</u>*—set in San Francisco—was of more conventional length, but then again, it was written entirely in sonnets, including the acknowledgments, the dedication, and the list of chapters.

Wilder's _Bridge of San Luis Rey_ concerned the collapse of a Peruvian bridge in 1714.

The French novelist Pierre Boulle is best known now for two books that became even better-known films. _Planet of the Apes_ (1963) has much the same plot as the 1968 movie, except that the astronauts are French. His 1952 bestseller, however, was _The Bridge over the River Kwai_, filmed under the title _The Bridge on the River Kwai_. Boulle won an Oscar for the film's screenplay in 1957, although it was actually written by Michael Wilson and Carl Foreman—who were both blacklisted at the time as Communists. (Boulle himself could neither write nor speak English and didn't turn up for the ceremony.) They finally received their own Academy Awards for it in 1984, posthumously.

Robert Kincaid and Francesca Johnson are the two lovers at the center of _The Bridges of Madison County_, that enormous bestseller of the 1990s by Robert James Waller.

3. BIRDS

Jean Louise Finch is better known as "Scout" Finch and is therefore the narrator of _To Kill a Mockingbird_.

Beau Geste is a much-filmed novel by P. C. Wren, set in the French Foreign Legion.

"Hail to thee" etc. is the first line of Percy Bysshe Shelley's "To a Skylark."

Iain Banks's 1992 novel was _The Crow_ Road, which

has one of the more striking first lines in literature: "It was the day my grandmother exploded."

4. BURNED BOOKS

On its publication in 1915, D. H. Lawrence's *Rainbow* was seized by the police, declared obscene and banned. More than a thousand copies were then burned by order of the examining magistrate.

Erich Maria Remarque's antiwar novel *All Quiet on the Western Front* was one of the books publicly burned by the Nazis in 1933—although in a happy Hollywood ending, Remarque escaped to America and later married the actress Paulette Goddard.

At the height of the *Satanic Verses* controversy, copies of Salman Rushdie's novel were publicly burned by some Muslim groups.

Finally, in one of literary history's most poignant mishaps, Carlyle lent the only manuscript of the first volume of *The French Revolution* to his friend John Stuart Mill. Mill's housemaid then found it by the fender and used it to light the fire. Rather heroically, after Mill had broken the news, Carlyle told his wife: "The poor fellow is terribly cut up. We must endeavour to hide from him how serious this business is to us." In fact, Carlyle was devastated—not least because he'd kept no notes and was broke at the time. It took him six months to rewrite the burned book. "I seem to myself," he told his journal when he'd finished, "like a man that had nearly worn the Life out of him, accomplishing—*zero*."

Round Five

No First Names Here: An Initials Round

1. A. A. Milne. (The poem is "Jonathan Jo," from *When We Were Very Young*.)

2. D. M. Thomas

3. E. E. Cummings (or possibly e. e. cummings)

4. H. L. Mencken

5. H. P. Lovecraft

6. J. M. Barrie—who took the first name of Wendy Darling in *Peter Pan* from Margaret Emma Henley, a little girl who used to call Barrie her "frendy-wendy." (Wendy had been known as a boys' name before that.)

7. P. D. James

8. V. I. Warshawski, as created by Sara Paretsky

9. W. B. Yeats. The house was on Chalcot Road, London, and her flat occupied the top two floors.

10. W. H. Auden. In the movie, Matthew (John Hannah) reads the poem "Funeral Blues"—the one beginning "Stop all the clocks"—over the coffin of his lover Gareth (Simon Callow). The scene caused Auden's sales to soar.

Quiz Four

Round One

It's War!

1. Which American poet wrote the so-called *Pisan Cantos* while being held as a prisoner in Italy by the American army?

2. Who wrote the series of novels set in the Royal Navy during the Napoleonic wars, and featuring Horatio Hornblower?

3. Which 1959 novel features Americans who'd been brainwashed during the Korean War?

4. Which nonfiction bestseller, first published in 1993, contains a torture scene set in Iraq's Abu Ghraib prison?

5. Which classic novel of World War II begins: "It was love at first sight"?

6. Who covered the first Gulf War in his characteristically titled book *Give War a Chance*?

7. Who wrote the classic of the Vietnam War, *The Things They Carried*?

8. In which war did Lord Byron die?

9. Which trilogy of plays, first performed in 1931, updated Aeschylus's Oresteia to the American Civil War?

10. In Homer's *Iliad*, who kills Hector?

Answers on p. 107

Round Two

A Little Bit of Politics

1. The first part of an open letter to the president, from a bestselling book of 2001, although the author is perhaps better known in another branch of the arts.

Q4

   I would like to ask you three pointed questions—and I would like you to give me, and the American people, three honest answers.

   1. George, are you able to read and write on an adult level?

   It appears to me and many others that, sadly, you may be a functional illiterate. This is nothing to be ashamed of. Millions of Americans cannot read and write above a fourth-grade level. But if you have trouble comprehending the complex position papers you are handed as the Leader of Mostly-Free World, how can we entrust something like our nuclear secrets to you?

   All the signs of illiteracy are there. The first clue was what you named as your favorite childhood book. "*The Very Hungry Caterpillar*," you said.

   Unfortunately, that book wasn't even published until a year after you graduated from college . . .

2. From a writer's autobiography of 1987:

   The ease with which I could, in the sixties, understand the fear and frustration of the dissident in the

Sovietized world was the result, in some great part, of my experience before the Un-American Activities Committee in the fifties.

A Cincinnati congressman named Gordon Scherer sternly asked whether "a Communist who is a poet should have the right to advocate the overthrow of this government by force and violence?" (He was probably unaware that nobody read poets in America except other poets and students under compulsion.) When I confirmed that I did think a poet could legally write such a subversive poem, Mr. Scherer actually threw up his hands and turned to the other members as though to say, "What more do we have to ask?"

Marilyn had come to give me moral support during the last days of the hearing. It had never been easy for me to share trouble with a woman. I was protecting a wound, but she glimpsed herself an unwanted wife.

3. Which Nobel Laureate is this speaking on his seventy-fifth birthday, which he celebrated with a visit to the Soviet Union in 1931? (The two points, then, are just for the author here.)

We don't know how to adequately express our gratitude for all that your country's Communist government has done for us. It's a real comfort to me, an old man, to be able to step into my grave with the knowledge that the civilization of the world will be saved. It is here in Russia that I have actually been convinced that the new Communist system is capable of leading mankind out of its present crisis, and saving it from complete anarchy and ruin.

4. The term opened vigorously as usual. – – stood bronzed before her class and said, "I have spent most of my summer holidays in Italy once more, and I have brought back a great many pictures which we can pin on the wall. Here is a larger formation of Mussolini's fascisti, it is a better view of them than that of last year's picture. They are doing splendid things as I shall tell you later. I went with my friends for an audience with the Pope. I wore a long black gown with a lace mantilla, and looked magnificent. Mussolini is one of the greatest men in the world, far more so than Ramsay MacDonald.

Q4

The last two political extracts here are by the two people whose names came up most often (certainly in Britain) if you searched for "America's greatest living writer" on the Internet—until 2009, when one of them died. In both cases, the passages chosen should be a solid clue to the books' titles—especially as the first one is the opening paragraph of the novel, setting the scene for what follows.

5. I remember I was sitting among my abandoned children watching television when Nixon resigned. My wife was out on a date, and had asked me to babysit. This was, of course, August. Nixon, with his bulgy face and his menacing, slipped-cog manner, seemed about to cry. The children and I had never seen a president resign before; nobody in the history of the United States had ever seen that.

6. It was the summer in America when the joking didn't stop, when the speculation and the theorizing and

Answers on p. 110

the hyperbole didn't stop, when some kind of demon had been unleashed in the nation and, on both sides, people wondered "Why are we so crazy?" when men and women alike discovered that during the night, they had dreamed of the brazenness of Bill Clinton. I myself dreamed of a mammoth banner, draped from one end of the White House to the other and bearing the legend A HUMAN BEING LIVES HERE. It was the summer when a president's penis was on everyone's mind, and life, in all its shameless impurity, once again confounded America.

Answer on p. 110

Round Three

Featured Author: J. K. Rowling

1. According to Rowling, which Harry Potter character is based partly on her as a girl?

2. What is J. K. Rowling's middle name?

3. What was the name of the first Harry Potter book?

4. When Harry first goes to Hogwarts Academy, who's the deputy head?

5. As whom is Tom Marvolo Riddle better known?

6. What are the first names of Harry's parents?

7. Which is the longest of the Harry Potter books?

8. In 2003, which Rowling-related word entered the *Oxford English Dictionary* to mean "a person who lacks a particular skill or skills—or who is regarded as inferior in some way"?

9. In 2004, *Forbes* magazine hailed Rowling as the first *what* in literary history?

10. Within 2 million either way, in the first twenty-four hours of publication, how many copies were sold worldwide of *Harry Potter and the Deathly Hallows*, the last book in the series?

     Answers on p. 111

Round Four

A Round on the Links: Literary Connections

Can you link the following literary people or things?

1. Frances Hodgson Burnett's Cedric Errol

   E. B. White's first book for children

   Miss St. Clair in a hugely bestselling and influential novel of 1852

   The long-awaited follow-up to *The Secret History*

2. The bestselling novel in America in 1931, and 1932

   John Gray (twice over)

   W. G. Sebald's rings

   Alice Munro's moons

3. Thomas de Quincey

   St. Augustine

   Paris Hilton

   William Styron

4. Rachel Carson in 1962

   Tennessee Williams, suddenly

   An Albert Camus novel set in Amsterdam

   A James Goldman play set in medieval Europe

101   Answers on pp. 113–116

Round Five

Animal Farm: A Zoological Round

All the answers here contain or comprise the name of an animal.

1. What kind of animal is Beatrix Potter's Jeremy Fisher?

Q4

2. What's the title of the bestselling 1969 book for young children by Eric Carle?

3. Still with children's books, who's the most famous literary creation of Jean de Brunhoff?

4. How is the Greek playwright Aeschylus traditionally said to have died?

5. Whose first novel of 1992 follows Dolores Price from the age of four to adulthood?

6. Which 1937 novel features the itinerant laborers George and Lennie?

7. What's the only Shakespeare play with an animal in the title?

8. Which Margaret Atwood novel concerns a painter called Elaine Risley returning to Toronto?

9. Which novel by Julia Alvarez is a fictional account of the real-life Mirabal sisters?

10. What's the first novel in Cormac McCarthy's Border trilogy?

Quiz Four: Answers

Round One

It's War!

1. Ezra Pound

2. C. S. Forester

3. *The Manchurian Candidate* by Richard Condon

4. *Bravo Two-Zero* by Andy McNab

5. *Catch-22* by Joseph Heller. The love is Yossarian's for the Air Force chaplain.

6. P. J. O'Rourke

7. Tim O'Brien

8. The Greek War of Independence—although he died of a fever before seeing any serious military action

9. *Mourning Becomes Electra* by Eugene O'Neill

10. Achilles

A4

Round Two

A Little Bit of Politics

1. A characteristically understated passage from *Stupid White Men* by Michael Moore—where the other two questions are "George, are you an alcoholic?" and "George, are you a felon?"

A4

2. From *Timebends* by Arthur Miller. The activities of the HUAC, of course, inspired Miller's play *The Crucible*—and, of course, too, the Marilyn there was his then-wife, Marilyn Monroe. Elsewhere, the book contains a vivid description of the effect her beauty had on him when they first met. "The sight of her was something like pain," Miller writes, "and I knew I must flee or walk into a doom beyond all knowing." Understandably, he opted for the doom.

3. That was George Bernard Shaw speaking at Moscow's Trade Union Central Hall—the same hall that his host Stalin would soon be using for show trials. During his trip, as Michael Holroyd's biography explains, Shaw also "congratulated Soviet citizens engaged in compulsory labour on working for public service and not for the private profit of a few individuals: 'I wish we had forced labour in England,' he added, 'in which case we would not have 2,000,000 unemployed.'" Other Soviet celebrations for the great man's birthday included the Bernard Shaw Handicap at a nearby

race course—although, for the record, Shaw didn't actually step into his grave for another nineteen years. Stalin, says Holroyd, later complained to his daughter that Shaw was "an awful person."

Another of Shaw's great (and equally doomed) causes was spelling reform. After the atom bombs had been dropped on Japan, he wrote to the *Times* to protest—about the unnecessary "b" on the end of the word "bomb."

4. From Muriel Spark's *Prime of Miss Jean Brodie*— and the start of the autumn term of 1931 at Marcia Blaine School for Girls. Miss Brodie's fascist leanings later get her the sack, when she encourages Joyce Emily to fight for Franco in the Spanish Civil War.

5. From *Memories of the Ford Administration* by John Updike—where yet another suburban Updike adulterer reflects on his life, this time under the president who replaced Nixon. In the novel, in fact, Updike sees a lot of things in terms of presidential administrations—including one woman's navel, which showed that the "umbilicus had been cut in careless, Roosevelt-era style."

6. From *The Human Stain* by Philip Roth, set in the summer of 1998. The novel was the third of that loose trilogy, in which the three books are all narrated by Nathan Zuckerman, all concern the effect of American history on individuals, and all are centered on years with an "8" at the end. The previous two were *American Pastoral*, set in 1968, and *I Married a Communist*, set in 1948.

Round Three

Featured Author: J. K. Rowling

A4

1. Hermione Granger

2. She doesn't have one. When her publishers suggested that the name "Joanne Rowling" might turn boy readers away and that she should go by her initials, she had to invent a middle initial—and so took "K" for Kathleen from her grandmother.

3. *Harry Potter and the Sorcerer's Stone*. (The British title was *Harry Potter and the Philosopher's Stone*.)

4. Professor Minerva McGonagall

5. Voldemort (or He Who Must Not Be Named)

6. James and Lily

7. *Harry Potter and the Order of the Phoenix*

8. Muggle—the word that Rowling's wizards use for non-wizards

9. Billionaire author

10. 15 million, breaking the world sales records that had been held in turn by each of Rowling's previous three books

Round Four

A Round on the Links: Literary Connections

1. THE WORD "LITTLE"

Cedric Errol is the sweet little boy from New York who finds out he's the heir to a British title and goes off to become <u>Little</u> Lord Fauntleroy in Frances Hodgson Burnett's 1886 novel of that name. The book's enormous success led to a widespread fashion among the middle classes for dressing their sons in velvet suits.

E. B. White—until then a poet, essayist, and *New Yorker* staff writer—turned to children's fiction in 1945 with *Stuart <u>Little</u>*. *Charlotte's Web* followed in 1952.

Eva St. Clair is known as <u>Little</u> Eva in *Uncle Tom's Cabin* by Harriet Beecher Stowe. At the end of her short but saintly life, she has a deathbed scene almost as lingering and sentimental as Little Nell's in Charles Dickens's *Old Curiosity Shop*.

Fans of Donna Tartt's first novel, *The Secret History*, had to wait ten years for her second, *The <u>Little</u> Friend*, published in 2002.

2. PLANETS

The bestselling American novel in both of those years was Pearl S. Buck's *Good <u>Earth</u>*, set in China, where Buck had grown up as the child of missionaries, and where she became a missionary herself. In 1938, her run of success continued when she became the first American woman to win the Nobel Prize for Literature. *The Good Earth* returned to the bestseller lists in 2004 when it was chosen for Oprah's Book Club.

John Gray's *Men Are from Mars, Women Are from Venus* is reckoned to be the bestselling relationship book ever published, with more than 40 million copies sold. Possibly as a result, Gray's later books have included *Mars and Venus in the Bedroom, Mars and Venus Together Forever, Mars and Venus in Love, Mars and Venus on a Date, Mars and Venus Starting Over, Practical Miracles for Mars and Venus, Truly Mars and Venus,* and *The Mars and Venus Diet and Exercise Solution.*

The Rings of Saturn (1998) was the second of W. G. Sebald's novels to be translated into English, following *The Emigrants* in 1996. With his critical reputation established but still growing, Sebald was killed in a car crash in 2001, at age fifty-seven.

The Moons of Jupiter was the fifth short-story collection by Alice Munro, three-time winner of Canada's most prestigious book prize, the Governor General's Literary Award for Fiction. According to Jonathan Franzen, Munro "has a strong claim to being the best fiction writer now working in North America." According to Cynthia Ozick, she is "our Chekhov."

3. CONFESSIONS

Thomas de Quincey made his name in 1822 with _Confessions of an English Opium Eater_—written when opium was as easily obtainable, and as legal, as aspirin is today. The book did much to draw attention to its dangers.

St. Augustine's _Confessions_ is often described as the first autobiography, as well as being the only fourth-century work of theology to appear in this book. It contains the popular prayer: "Oh, Master, make me chaste and celibate—but not yet!"

Paris Hilton's sort-of autobiography _Confessions of an Heiress_ was published in 2004—and, perhaps unexpectedly, there's now an online study guide to the book. ("In the first chapter, Paris explains that people seem to have many misconceptions about her, and that she wrote this book in order to give an honest view of who she really is. Being an heiress is not easy, Paris writes, but it is fun and exciting.")

William Styron won the 1968 Pulitzer Prize for Fiction with _The Confessions of Nat Turner_, his novelized account of a slave uprising in Virginia in 1831.

4. THE FOUR SEASONS

Rachel Carson was a popular writer on natural history before publishing _The Silent Spring_ in 1962, the pioneering work of environmentalism that in particular exposed the dangers of DDT and helped to bring about a ban on its use in America.

Suddenly, Last <u>Summer</u> by Tennessee Williams is a one-act play from 1958 dealing with such familiar Williams themes as madness and homosexuality—the second of which had to be toned down for the 1959 movie starring Montgomery Clift, Elizabeth Taylor, and Katharine Hepburn.

The <u>Fall</u> by Albert Camus is set in Amsterdam and deals with such familiar Camus themes as guilt, freedom, and the utter meaninglessness of human life.

The Lion in <u>Winter</u> by James Goldman features King Henry II of England, who at that time also ruled large parts of France, spending the Christmas of 1183 at his château in Chinon. In 1968, Goldman won the Oscar for best adapted screenplay for his film version—the year before his brother William won for best original screenplay with *Butch Cassidy and the Sundance Kid*.

Round Five

Animal Farm: A Zoological Round

1. A frog

2. *The Very Hungry Caterpillar*—George W. Bush's favorite, as featured in Round Two

3. Babar the Elephant

4. When an eagle dropped a tortoise on his head—the story being that the bird mistook Aeschylus's bald head for a rock

5. Wally Lamb's. (The novel was *She's Come Undone*.)

6. *Of Mice and Men* by John Steinbeck

7. *The Taming of the Shrew*

8. *Cat's Eye*

9. *In the Time of Butterflies*

10. *All the Pretty Horses*

A4

117

Quiz Five

Round One

Book Bindings: Literature and Marriage

1. Which bestselling Irish author wrote the novel *Lucy Sullivan Is Getting Married*?

2. What's the title of Joan Didion's book about the death of her husband, John Gregory Dunne?

3. Which nineteenth-century literary character marries Isabella Linton?

4. In Chaucer's *Canterbury Tales*, how many times had the Wife of Bath been married?

5. Which of these writers had the most marriages: Ernest Hemingway, Norman Mailer, or Saul Bellow?

6. Who wrote the 1998 novel *The Pilot's Wife*?

7. Whose last and unfinished novel was *Wives and Daughters*?

8. Which Spanish dramatist wrote *Blood Wedding*?

9. Whose first novel was *The World Is Full of Married Men*?

10. Who depicted a particularly poisonous marriage in his play *The Dance of Death*?

Q5

Answers on p. 135

Round Two

How Do You Do: First Appearances of Famous Characters

The following passages all contain the moment when what proved to be an unforgettable new literary creation was introduced to the world. In all cases, please identify the character, the book, and the author—for one point each. This round also divides neatly into three villains, followed by three sexpots. (And, just to get you started, for the first villain you should note his keen interest in food.)

Q5

1. Steel bars covered the entire front of the cell. Behind the bars, farther than arm's reach, was a stout nylon net stretched ceiling to floor and wall to wall. Through the barrier, Graham could see a table and chair bolted to the floor.

   The man lay on his cot asleep. His head propped on a pillow against the wall. Alexandre Dumas's *Le Grand Dictionnaire de Cuisine* was open on his chest.

   Graham had stared through the bars for about five seconds when the man opened his eyes and said. "That's some atrocious aftershave you wore in court."

   The man's eyes are maroon and they reflect the light redly in tiny points. Graham felt each hair bristle on his nape.

2. At that moment, the peace was shattered by an extremely strident motor horn. A large car was

     Answers on p. 137

coming towards them. It drew up at a big house just ahead of them and a tall woman came out on to the front-door steps. She was wearing a tight-fitting emerald satin dress, several ropes of rubies, and an absolutely simple white mink cloak, which reached to the high heels of her ruby-red shoes. She had a dark skin, black eyes with a tinge of red in them, and a very pointed nose. Her hair was parted severely down the middle and one half of it was black and the other white—rather unusual.

3. I heard a heavy step approaching behind the great door, and saw through the chinks the gleam of a coming light. Then there was the sound of rattling chains and the clanking of massive bolts drawn back. A key was turned with the loud grating noise of long disuse, and the great door swung back.

Within stood a tall old man, clean shaven save for a long white moustache, and clad in black from head to foot, without a single speck of colour about him anywhere. He motioned me in with his right hand with a courtly gesture, saying in excellent English, but with a strange intonation:—

"Welcome to my house! Enter freely and of your own will!"

And so to the first appearances of the sexy characters, beginning with this heroine, who's about to be embarrassed by her old dad . . .

4. She was a fine and handsome girl—not handsomer than some others, possibly—but her mobile peony mouth and large innocent eyes added eloquence to

colour and shape. She wore a red ribbon in her hair, and was the only one of the company who could boast of such a pronounced adornment. As she looked round her father was seen moving along the road in a chaise belonging to the Pure Drop Inn, driven by a frizzle-haired brawny damsel. Leaning back, and with his eyes closed luxuriously, he was waving his hand above his head, and singing in a slow recitative—

"I've-got-a-gr't-family-vault-at-Kingsbere—and knighted-forefathers-in-lead-coffins-there!"

5. Here, in translation, two people meet who will later become lovers. But who's the woman with the impressive eyelashes—and whose name is also the title of the novel? One final clue: the location of the meeting turns out to be ironically significant . . .

Q5

He followed the guard to the carriage, and at the door of the compartment had to stop and make way for a lady who was getting out. His experience as a man of the world told him at a glance that she belonged to the best society. He begged her pardon and was about to enter the carriage but felt he must have another look at her—not on account of the elegance and unassuming grace of her whole figure, but because of something tender and caressing in her lovely face as she passed him. As he looked round, she, too, turned her head. Her brilliant grey eyes, shadowed by thick lashes, gave him a friendly, attentive look. In that brief glance he had time to notice the suppressed animation which played over

125   Answers on p. 138

her face and flitted between her sparkling eyes and
the slight smile curving her red lips.

6. Finally in this round, here's a sexpot for the
   ladies—from a novel that became a (posthumously)
   huge bestseller in Britain for a very specific reason.

   She was watching a brown spaniel that had run out
   of a side-path, and was looking towards them with
   lifted nose, making a soft, fluffy bark. A man with a
   gun strode swiftly, softly out after the dog, facing
   their way as if about to attack them; then stopped
   instead, saluted, and was turning downhill. He had
   frightened her, he seemed to emerge with such a
   swift menace. That was how she had seen him, like
   the sudden rush of a threat out of nowhere.
   He was a man in dark green velveteens and
   gaiters . . . the old style, with a red face and red
   moustache and distant eyes. He was moderately tall
   and lean, and was silent. He did not look at her at
   all, only at the chair.

Answers on p. 138   126

Round Three

Featured Author: John le Carré

1. What is John le Carré's real name?

2. Le Carré's breakthrough novel was his third, published in 1963. What was it called?

3. How does the title of a 1971 le Carré novel refer to its main character, Aldo Cassidy? (The novel wasn't a spy book and, maybe as a result, was a serious commercial flop.)

4. "The best English novel since the war" was Philip Roth's verdict on which le Carré book—according to le Carré himself, his most autobiographical?

5. *Smiley's People* was the third book in a trilogy that began with which novel?

6. Which country is the main setting for le Carré's *The Constant Gardener*?

7. What's the first name of George Smiley's unfaithful wife?

8. Why were le Carré and his wife in central London on February 15, 2003?

9. Who did le Carré once say was motivated only by "the self-hate of a vain misfit for whom nothing will ever be worthy of his loyalty"?

10. In *Tinker, Tailor, Soldier, Spy*, what's the code name for the mole?

Answers on pp. 139–140

Round Four

A Round on the Links: Literary Connections

Can you link the following literary people or things?

1. The best-known story in Annie Proulx's *Close Range: Wyoming Stories*

   Thomas Mann's Hans Castorp

   Inman returns from the American Civil War in Charles Frazier's first novel

   Jean Craighead George in 1959

2. "The Road Not Taken" (a poem)

   Strangers and Brothers (an eleven-novel sequence)

   The man who circled the globe in approximately 115,200 minutes (with a small spelling change)

   Richard Hughes's novel of Jamaica

3. Paul Auster's *City of Glass*

   Chester Himes's rage

   John Dos Passos's transfer

   The Red and White characters who ask Alice a series of riddles in Lewis Carroll's *Through the Looking Glass*

4. (Professionally speaking:)

   Mao Tse-tung

Giacomo Casanova

Dee Brown

Jorge Luis Borges

Answer on pp. 143–144

Round Five

The Rainbow: A Colorful Round

All the answers here contain the name of a color.

1. Brachiano is one of the main characters in which play by John Webster?

2. Which enduring classic of 1857 was written by Thomas Hughes?

Q5

3. As whom is Anne Shirley better known in a 1908 novel by L. M. Montgomery?

4. In which 1983 novel does the narrator Celie tell of her love for Shug Avery?

5. Who wrote one of the earliest Westerns, *The Riders of the Purple Sage*? (And here it might help to know your British spellings.)

6. In which nineteenth-century American classic is the main character Hester Prynne?

7. In which nineteenth-century American classic is the main character Henry Fleming, a Civil War soldier?

8. Name any Iris Murdoch novel with a color in the title.

9. Which book of 1877 is described on the title page as having been "translated from the original equine"?

10. In the poem by Edward Lear, in what kind of vessel do the owl and the pussycat go to sea?

     Answers on p. 145

Quiz Five: Answers

Round One

Book Bindings: Literature and Marriage

1. Marian Keyes

2. *The Year of Magical Thinking*

3. Heathcliff—in Emily Brontë's *Wuthering Heights*

4. Five—and her husbands are all dead. ("The first three men were good, and rich, and old.")

5. Norman Mailer—with six. Bellow was married five times, and Hemingway four.

6. Anita Shreve

7. Elizabeth Gaskell's

8. Federico García Lorca

9. Jackie Collins

10. August Strindberg

A5

Round Two

How Do You Do: First Appearances of Famous Characters

1. The first appearance of Dr. Hannibal Lecter, in *Red Dragon* by Thomas Harris. Lecter is a relatively minor character in that book—but went on to play a much bigger role in Harris's later novels, *The Silence of the Lambs*, *Hannibal*, and *Hannibal Rising*. He's also, surely, one of the few people in the whole of fiction with maroon eyes.

2. That was Mr. and Mrs. Dearly looking on as Cruella de Vil comes out to meet her chauffeur in *The Hundred and One Dalmatians* by Dodie Smith. In the next paragraph, Mrs. Dearly gives her husband some alarming background information. "Why, that's Cruella de Vil," she says. "We were at school together. She was expelled for drinking ink."

3. The big entrance of Count Dracula, in Bram Stoker's *Dracula*—with Jonathan Harker becoming the first person ever to hear the heavy footsteps coming toward that Transylvanian castle door and all those bolts being drawn back. In fact, most of the characteristics of the movie *Dracula* were already present and correct in the original novel— apart from that long white moustache. And two pages later, after a nice supper, the Count really does hear some wolves and say, "The children of the night. What music they make!"

4. Thomas Hardy introducing us to Tess of the d'Urbervilles—or simple Tess Durbeyfield as she is then. Her father's head has just been turned by discovering he is related to the great d'Urberville family of Kingsbere—which sort of leads to Tess being seduced, giving birth to an illegitimate baby who dies, stabbing her lover, being hanged for the crime, and so on.

5. Vronsky bumping into Anna Karenina in Leo Tolstoy's novel. First seen on a train, Anna ends up throwing herself under one.

6. From *Lady Chatterley's Lover* by D. H. Lawrence. Lady Constance Chatterley is walking with her wheelchair-bound husband when they meet the new gamekeeper, one Oliver Mellors. After the novel was prosecuted unsuccessfully for obscenity in Britain in 1960, and Penguin was free to publish the unexpurgated version, it sold 200,000 copies on the first day—and around 2 million more in the next six weeks. At one point in the trial, the chief prosecutor, Mervyn Griffith-Jones, asked the jury (three of whom were women) if this were "the sort of book you'd wish your wife or servants to read"—a remark that has been ridiculed ever since. In the United States, the ban on the novel was over-turned in 1959.

Round Three

Featured Author: John le Carré

1. David Cornwell

2. *The Spy Who Came in from the Cold*

3. *The Naïve and Sentimental Lover*

4. *A Perfect Spy*

5. *Tinker, Tailor, Soldier, Spy*. (The second was *The Honourable Schoolboy*.)

6. Kenya

7. Ann

8. They were at a demonstration against the Iraq war. Just before the war began, le Carré also wrote an essay starkly titled "The United States Has Gone Mad." ("How Bush and his junta succeeded in deflecting America's anger from bin Laden to Saddam Hussein is one of the great public relations conjuring tricks of history," he wrote.)

9. Kim Philby. Actually this is one of his milder remarks about Philby—the double agent who, according to some sources, was responsible for ending le Carré's own career in the British secret service by revealing to the Russians that he was a spy. Either way, in 2000, le Carré explained that

Philby had "carried to the grave my unqualified contempt."

10. Gerald. The mole (whose real name can't possibly be divulged here) was largely based on Philby.

Round Four

A Round on the Links: Literary Connections

1. MOUNTAINS

Despite the fact that the other tales have such memorable titles as "The Half-Skinned Steer," "55 Miles to the Gas Pump," and "People in Hell Just Want a Drink of Water," the most famous story in *Close Range* has got to be "Brokeback Mountain"— about, as you may know, the love between two cowboys.

A5

Hans Castorp is the main character in Mann's *Magic Mountain*, set in a sanatorium in the Swiss Alps.

Inman, whose first name we never learn, is the protagonist of Frazier's *Cold Mountain* (1997).

My Side of the Mountain (1959), set in the Catskills, is one of more than one hundred books for children by Jean Craighead George—and not to be confused with the 1990 sequel, *The Far Side of the Mountain*.

2. BAD WEATHER (OR, ALTERNATIVELY, HAZARDOUS DRIVING CONDITIONS)

"The Road Not Taken" is the poem by Robert <u>Frost</u> that contains the lines, "I took the one less traveled by,/ And that has made all the difference."

Strangers and Brothers is by C. P. <u>Snow</u>. The ninth novel in the series, by the way, is *Corridors of Power*, a phrase Snow had coined in the sixth, *Homecomings*—and which had already caught on. (In the foreword to *Corridors of Power* he expresses the hope that he's entitled to use his own cliché.)

Phileas <u>Fogg</u> is the main character in Jules Verne's *Around the World in Eighty Days*, whose title was so cunningly disguised there. Incidentally, Fogg never travels by hot-air balloon in the novel. Still, the fact that he briefly considers it at one point was good enough for Hollywood—which is why most people (especially the advertisers of hot-air balloon trips) tend to imagine that he did.

With its unsentimental view of a group of unsupervised children, Richard Hughes's 1929 novel *A <u>High Wind</u> in Jamaica* is sometimes said to prefigure *Lord of the Flies*. The 1965 film version featured an appearance from the young Martin Amis, who by his own account, "talentlessly played one of the children." In the finished movie, his voice was dubbed by an elderly woman.

3. NEW YORK

City of Glass is the first part of Paul Auster's <u>New York</u> trilogy, the other two being *Ghosts* and *The Locked Room*.

Chester Himes's *A Rage in <u>Harlem</u>* was the first of his hard-boiled crime novels set among black New Yorkers.

John Dos Passos was one of America's most highly regarded novelists in the 1920s and '30s, and although his reputation has maybe declined a bit since, his 1925 novel _Manhattan Transfer_ was still famous enough to give its name to a leading vocal group of the 1970s and '80s.

In Chapter 9 of _Through the Looking Glass_, it's the Red and White <u>Queens</u> who pose those riddles to Alice, some of them reflecting Lewis Carroll's other life as the Reverend Charles Dodgson, an Oxford professor of mathematics. (One of the books he wrote between the two Alice novels was enticingly called _Elementary Treatise on Determinants, With Their Application to Simultaneous Linear Equations and Algebraical Geometry._)

4. THEY WERE ALL LIBRARIANS

As a young graduate, Mao worked in a university library and qualifies as a writer because his _Little Red Book_ is one of the bestselling books ever. Its sales were helped by the fact that it was compulsory for every Chinese citizen to own a copy and to carry it at all times.

Casanova anticlimactically spent the last thirteen years of his life as a librarian in what's now the Czech Republic—which is when and where he wrote his scandalous autobiography.

During the Great Depression, Dee Brown left his native Arkansas and went to find a job in Washington, DC, becoming a librarian in the U.S. Department of Agriculture. After that, he continued as a librarian, and when *Bury My Heart at Wounded Knee* was published in 1970, he was working at the College of Agriculture library at the University of Illinois in Urbana-Champaign. The book went on to sell more than 5 million copies, marking a turning point in public awareness of the fate of Native Americans in the nineteenth century.

Borges, who generally appears on all those lists of writers who should have won the Nobel Prize, was first a municipal librarian and eventually the Director of the National Library in Buenos Aires. He resigned when Juan Perón was re-elected President of Argentina in 1973.

Round Five

The Rainbow: A Colorful Round

1. *The <u>White</u> Devil*

2. *Tom <u>Brown</u>'s Schooldays*

3. Anne of <u>Green</u> Gables

4. *The Color <u>Purple</u>* by Alice Walker

5. Zane <u>Grey</u>

6. *The <u>Scarlet</u> Letter* by Nathaniel Hawthorne. Hester is forced by her New England puritan community to wear the scarlet letter itself: an A for adultery.

7. *The <u>Red</u> Badge of Courage* by Stephen Crane

8. *The <u>Black</u> Prince*; *The <u>Green</u> Knight*; *The <u>Red</u> and the <u>Green</u>*. (*An Unofficial <u>Rose</u>* would also be acceptable.)

9. *<u>Black</u> Beauty* by Anna Sewell

10. A beautiful <u>pea green</u> boat

Quiz Six

Round One

Devouring Books: Literary Food and Drink

1. Who wrote the poem containing the phrase, "Sandalwood, cedarwood, and sweet white wine"?

2. In Anne Rice's Vampire Chronicles, what's the name of the vampire?

3. In George Orwell's *Nineteen Eighty-Four*, how is the nightmare totalitarian future reflected in the way beer is served?

4. Whose first novel was *The Dud Avocado*?

5. Which 2006 bestseller is subtitled *One Woman's Search for Everything Across Italy, India and Indonesia*?

6. What's the first line of *Green Eggs and Ham* by Dr. Seuss?

7. Which novel of 1906 did much to change conditions in the American meat-packing industry?

8. A taste of which foodstuff prompted the original Proustian rush?

9. According to his own doctor, which French novelist, author of *Le Père Goriot* and *Le Cousin Pons*, died of caffeine poisoning?

10. What's the connection between coffee and Captain Ahab's first mate in *Moby-Dick*?

Q6

 Answers on p. 163

Round Two

Dear Sir or Madam: Literature and Letters

In this round, the two points for the answer work in a variety of ways, which I'll explain in each question.

1. The person who wrote this 1893 letter must later have come to regret that he did. Who is he, and who is he writing to, for one point each?

    My Own Boy,
        Your sonnet is quite lovely, and it is a marvel that those red rose-leaf lips of yours should have been made no less for music of song than for madness of kisses. Your slim gilt soul walks between passion and poetry. I know Hyacinthus, whom Apollo loved so madly, was you in Greek days.
        Come here whenever you like. It is a lovely place—it only lacks you.
        Always, with undying love, yours . . .

2. In this extraordinarily sad letter from 1848, can you name both the writer and the person being written about, for one point each? For the writer, you may find yourself torn in three directions—but the (admittedly tough) clue is meant to be the phrase "a year my junior."

    My Dear Sir
        A lull begins to succeed the gloomy tumult of last week. It is not permitted us to grieve for him who is

gone as others grieve for those they lose. I do not weep from a sense of bereavement—there is no prop withdrawn, no consolation torn away, no dear companion lost—but for the wreck of talent, the ruin of promise, the untimely dreary extinction of what might have been a burning and a shining light. My brother was a year my junior. I had aspirations and ambitions for him once, long ago—they have perished mournfully. Nothing remains of him but a memory of errors and sufferings.

My unhappy brother never knew what his sisters had done in literature—he was never aware that they had ever published a line. We could not tell him of our own efforts for fear of causing him too deep a pang of remorse for his own time misspent, and talents misapplied. Now he will never know.

3. This 1812 letter put a crunching end to one of literary history's most notoriously tempestuous love affairs—and also contains a savage twist to the traditional line about hoping to stay friends. Who wrote the letter, and who was its unfortunate recipient, for one point each?

My dear lady

I am no longer your lover; and since you oblige me to confess it by this truly unfeminine persecution, learn that I am attached to another, whose name it would of course be dishonourable to mention. I shall ever remember with gratitude the many instances I have received of the predilection you have shown in my favour. I shall ever continue your friend, if your ladyship will permit me so to style myself; and as proof of my regard, I offer you this advice: correct your vanity, which is ridiculous; exert your absurd caprices upon others; and leave me in peace.

4. Here's a fairly ungallant description of a major female writer—from an 1869 letter by a young American who'd just visited her. Later he'd become as famous a novelist as she was, and settle permanently in England. Please name them both for one point each.

> She is magnificently ugly—deliciously hideous. She has a low forehead, a dull gray eye, a vast pendulous nose, a huge mouth full of uneven teeth, and a chin and jawbone *qui n'en finissent pas*. In this vast ugliness resides a most powerful beauty which, in a very few minutes, steals forth and charms the mind, so that you end as I ended, in falling in love with her. Yes behold me literally in love with this great horse-faced blue-stocking. Altogether, she has a larger circumference than any woman I have ever seen.

Q6

5. The beginning of a perhaps unlikely friendship now. The recipient isn't hard to spot here—so for two points you just need to identify which towering twentieth-century poet wrote this, in response to a get-well-soon note?

> Dear Groucho Marx
>
>   It seems more of an impertinence to address Groucho Marx as "Dear Mr. Marx" than it would be to address any other celebrity by his first name. It is out of respect, my dear Groucho, that I address you as I do. This is to thank you for your letter and to say

that I am convalescing as fast as the awful winter weather permits, that my wife and I hope to get to Bermuda next month for warmth and fresh air and to be back in London in time to greet you in the spring.

Will Mrs. Groucho be with you? You ought to bring a secretary, a public relations official and a couple of private detectives, to protect you from the London press; but we hope you will give us the honour of taking a meal with us.

PS. Your portrait is framed on my office mantelpiece.

6. Finally, from 1925, a letter from one American literary giant to another that sums them both up nicely. Who are they, for one point each?

I'm feeling better than I've ever felt—haven't drunk anything but wine since I left Paris. I wonder what your idea of heaven would be—A beautiful vacuum filled with wealthy monogamists, all powerful and members of the best families, all drinking themselves to death.

To me heaven would be a big bull ring with me holding two barrera seats and a trout stream outside that no one else was allowed to fish in and two lovely houses in the town: one where I would have my wife and children and be monogamous and love them truly and well, and the other where I would have my nine beautiful mistresses on 9 different floors.

Answers on p. 166

Round Three

Featured Author: John Keats

1. What's the celebrated first line of Keats's longest poem, "Endymion"?

2. What's the third word of the poem "To Autumn"?

3. Within two inches either way, how tall was the adult Keats?

4. In perhaps his worst early poem, to whom is Keats referring in these lines?

   God! She is like a milk-white lamb that bleats
   For man's protection

   Q6

5. Which Keats ode begins: "My heart aches"?

6. In 1819, who became Keats's fiancée?

7. Which poem contains the line, "And no birds sing"?

8. How old was Keats when he died?

9. What phrase was written, at his own request, on Keats's tombstone in Rome?

10. What was the title of Percy Bysshe Shelley's fifty-five-stanza elegy on Keats, published in 1821?

Answers on p. 167

Round Four

A Round on the Links: Literary Connections

Can you link the following literary people or things?

1. The last story in James Joyce's *Dubliners*

   The first Mrs. Rochester—but in a novel of 1966

   Stendhal's 1830 masterpiece (twice over)

   The fourth of the *Chronicles of Narnia*

2. (If it helps, this link is sort of linked to the previous link.)

   Half of Iris Murdoch's only Booker Prize winner

   Frank Herbert's bestselling sci-fi series

   Virginia Woolf's 1931 stream-of-consciousness novel, tracing a group of friends from childhood to late middle age

   Together, the detectives from *Bleak House* and *The Maltese Falcon*

3. Alex and his droogs speaking Nadsat

   Fannie Flagg in 1987

   The Joad family flees the Oklahoma dustbowl

   The Japanese author of *Kitchen, Goodbye Tsugumi,* and *Amrita*

4. (The last link here is purely factual—between the writers, whom you need to identify first from their works.)

Kane and Abel

Don Quixote

The Brothers Karamazov

The Pilgrim's Progress

Round Five

Tales from the City: An Urban Round

All the answers here contain or comprise the name of a city—as ever, in a variety of ways.

1. Who wrote the bestselling novel about the Kennedy assassination *The Death of a President*?

2. Which Evelyn Waugh novel, about the fourth-century search for Christ's cross, shares its name with an American state capital?

3. In the Broadway stories of Damon Runyon, who runs the floating crap game?

4. Which American city is the setting for almost all of the novels of Anne Tyler?

5. Which city is the setting for J. G. Ballard's autobiographical novel *The Empire of the Sun*?

6. "Oh death, where is thy sting?" is a quotation from which writer?

7. *The Letters of Peter Plymley* was an 1807 defense of Catholic emancipation by which much-quoted literary clergyman?

8. Which city is referred to in the title of Jonathan Franzen's first novel, *The Twenty-Seventh City*?

Q6

Answers on p. 173

9. In *The Firm* by John Grisham, in which city is the firm based?

10. With what novel did Ian McEwan win the 1998 Booker Prize?

Answers on p. 173

Quiz Six: Answers

Round One

Devouring Books: Literary Food and Drink

1. John Masefield. The poem is "Cargoes."

2. Lestat de Lioncourt

3. It's served in liters and half liters. Orwell was fiercely opposed to the metric system.

4. Elaine Dundy

5. *Eat, Pray, Love* by Elizabeth Gilbert

6. "That Sam-I-am!" (Which is also the second and fourth line.)

7. *The Jungle* by Upton Sinclair

8. A madeleine cake dipped in tea in Proust's *À la recherche du temps perdu*, which suddenly brought the narrator's memories of his childhood flooding back

9. Honoré de Balzac. Balzac drank coffee endlessly to fight what he saw as the pointless waste of time represented by sleep. As a result, he wrote the ninety-one novels in his *Comédie humaine* series in just twenty years—and died at fifty-one.

10. Captain Ahab's first mate is Starbuck—after whom the coffee chain is named, because the founders are fans of Melville's novel

Round Two

Dear Sir or Madam: Literature and Letters

1. Oscar Wilde writing to his lover Lord Alfred Douglas (aka "Bosie") from a family holiday in Babbacombe Cliff, Devon. The letter was later stolen by a blackmailer—and read out in court at Wilde's trials in 1895.

2. Charlotte Brontë writing to a publisher friend about her brother, Branwell, and definitely failing to sentimentalize his life in the light of his early death. Branwell, she says in the same letter, was "his father's and sisters' pride and hope in boyhood—but since manhood, the case has been otherwise." Both Anne and Emily were younger than their brother, although within nine months both of them were dead, too. And just to add to the cheerfulness of this question, Branwell was the model for the violent drunkard in Anne's novel, *The Tenant of Wildfell Hall*. (On a lighter note, as a young man he was once seduced by an older woman called Mrs. Robinson.)

3. That was Lord Byron leaving Lady Caroline Lamb in little doubt as to where she stood after an affair that, for all its continuing fame, lasted just five months. Lady Caroline, who famously called Byron "mad, bad, and dangerous to know," put the letter in her novel *Glenarvon*: a not-very-fictional

A6

account of their relationship, which became a hugely scandalous success in 1816.

The really bad news, though, is that Byron's letter didn't work. Two years after he wrote it, he complained to a friend that Lady Caroline "comes at all times, at any time, and the moment the door is open, in she walks. She has no shame, no feeling, no one estimable or redeemable quality."

4. The twenty-six-year-old Henry James writing to his father about George Eliot. In the letter, he did also acknowledge that it was a "marvel" someone so distinguished should have agreed to his visit at all. (At this stage he'd only published some reviews and short stories in American periodicals.) Nevertheless, in 1878, after another visit, he still seemed to have the same conflict about her appearance. Eliot, he told his brother William, "has a delightful expression" in "her large, long, pale equine face."

5. That was T. S. Eliot writing to Groucho Marx in the cold British winter of 1963. When the dinner between them finally happened, a year later, things turned out pretty much as you'd expect. Groucho studied up on *The Waste Land* and was keen to talk about literature. Eliot wanted to talk only about Marx Brothers' films and kept quoting jokes from them that Groucho couldn't remember. When Eliot died, Groucho wrote that, "He was a nice man—the best epitaph any man can have."

6. Ernest Hemingway in nicely relaxed form, writing from Spain to F. Scott Fitzgerald. Good to see there that Hemingway clearly regards drinking wine as not really drinking at all.

Round Three

Featured Author: John Keats

1. "A thing of beauty is a joy for ever"

2. "Mists"—as in "Season of mists and mellow fruit-fulness"

3. Five feet one inch. And that still makes him seven inches taller than the adult Alexander Pope.

4. Woman—from a poem beginning "Woman! When I behold thee flippant, vain." According to a friend, when Keats wrote those lines, he "burst into tears, overpowered by the tenderness of his own imagination." (To be fair, he was a teenager at the time.)

A6

5. "Ode to a Nightingale"

6. Fanny Brawne

7. "La Belle Dame sans Merci." (In fact, it contains it twice.)

8. Twenty-five. He died of tuberculosis in Rome in 1821.

9. "Here lies one whose name was writ in water"

10. "Adonais"—parts of which were read out loud by Mick Jagger at a Rolling Stones concert in London's Hyde Park after Brian Jones had died

Round Four

A Round on the Links: Literary Connections

1. SEAS

The last, longest, and most acclaimed story in Joyce's *Dubliners* is "The <u>Dead</u>"—as in, for our purposes, the Dead Sea.

The Wide <u>Sargasso</u> Sea is Jean Rhys's (kind of) prequel to *Jane Eyre*, and so concerns the early life in the Caribbean of the girl who ends up as Charlotte Brontë's mad woman in the attic.

Stendhal's 1830 novel is *The <u>Red</u> and the <u>Black</u>*—which are two seas, hence "twice over."

The fourth of C. S. Lewis's *The Chronicles of Narnia* is *Prince <u>Caspian</u>*—although, slightly confusingly, it was the second to be published.

2. THINGS YOU'D SEE AT THE SEASIDE

Iris Murdoch won the Booker Prize in 1978 for *The <u>Sea</u>, The Sea*.

Frank Herbert was the author of the multimillion-selling <u>Dune</u> chronicles, beginning with *Dune* itself, the bestselling science-fiction book ever.

Virginia Woolf's *The <u>Waves</u>* is her 1931 novel about that group of friends.

Inspector <u>Bucket</u> is the police inspector in Dickens's

Bleak House and Sam <u>Spade</u> is the private eye in Dashiell Hammett's *The Maltese Falcon*.

3. FRUIT

Nadsat is the language spoken by Alex and his teenage gang (known as droogs) in *A Clockwork <u>Orange</u>* by Anthony Burgess. The language draws heavily on Russian, with *nadsat* itself the Russian word for "teenager," and *droog* the Russian word for "friend."

It was in 1987 that Fannie Flagg published *Fried Green <u>Tomatoes</u> at the Whistle Stop Cafe*—and as the old saying has it, "Knowledge is knowing that a tomato is a fruit; wisdom is not putting it in a fruit salad."

The Joad family flees from that Oklahoma dustbowl to California in John Steinbeck's *<u>Grapes</u> of Wrath*.

Kitchen, *Goodbye Tsugumi*, and *Amrita* are three of the books by <u>Banana</u> Yoshimoto.

4. WRITERS WHO WENT TO PRISON

Kane and Abel was the third novel by Jeffrey Archer, who in 2001 was found guilty of perjury and perverting the course of justice. He served two years of a four-year sentence.

More romantically, Miguel de Cervantes—author of *Don Quixote*—was captured by pirates in 1575 and for the next five years was a prisoner in Algiers. (Later, back in Spain, he was imprisoned at least twice more for financial irregularities.)

In 1849, thirty-one years before publishing *The Brothers Karamazov*, Fyodor Dostoevsky was arrested for being part of a Socialist group and sent to a Siberian penal settlement for four years. His experiences in the camp were the basis of his book *Notes from the House of the Dead*—and also brought about a religious crisis that turned him from a Socialist into a Christian.

And speaking of Christians, from 1660 John Bunyan spent the best part of twelve years in Bedford jail for the serious crime of preaching without a license. While in prison, Bunyan wrote nine books and started on *The Pilgrim's Progress*, which he continued during another stint in prison in 1675.

A6

Round Five

Tales from the City: An Urban Round

1. William <u>Manchester</u>

2. *Helena*

3. Nathan <u>Detroit</u>. The stories are the basis of the musical *Guys and Dolls*.

4. Baltimore

5. Shanghai—where Ballard had been a boy during the Japanese invasion

6. St. Paul

7. <u>Sydney</u> Smith—Sydney with a "y," so he qualifies for this round

8. St. Louis—more specifically, the title refers to St. Louis's fall from being America's fourth biggest city in the nineteenth century to the twenty-seventh biggest by the late twentieth century

9. Memphis

10. *Amsterdam*

Quiz Seven

Round One

Books and the Arts

1. Which painter's household is the setting for Tracy Chevalier's novel *Girl with a Pearl Earring*?

2. Whose first novel was named after Elvis Costello's song *Less than Zero*?

3. Which 1960s band was named after a book by Aldous Huxley in praise of psychedelic drugs?

4. Which Nobel Prize–winning author co-wrote the screenplay for the 1945 film *To Have and Have Not*?

5. Which playwright played Cyril Kinnear in the film *Get Carter*?

6. Who wrote the 1992 novel *Jazz*?

7. What's the connection between the crime writer Patricia Cornwell and the painter Walter Sickert?

8. Which Samuel Beckett play shares its title with that of an American sitcom of the 1970s and '80s?

9. In 2004, which novelist unexpectedly appeared on *The Simpsons*, drawn with a paper bag over his head—but supplying his own voice?

10. Who wrote the eighteenth-century play *The Beggar's Opera*?

Q7

Answers on p. 191

Round Two

Pedants' Revolt: A Round of Literary Mistakes II

So yes, once again, in each of the following passages the author has made some technical or factual error. Can you identify the author, the work—and the mistake in question? (Once again, too, if you should happen to be quizzing seriously, there's one point for the book, one point for the author, and two for the mistake.)

1. The mistake here only becomes fully clear forty-one chapters later. Nonetheless, it definitely is one—and, given a bit of literary knowledge, can still be spotted from this dramatic passage:

    "Hold your noise!" cried a terrible voice, as a man started up from among the graves at the side of the church porch. "Keep still, you little devil, or I'll cut your throat!"

    A fearful man, all in coarse grey, with a great iron on his leg. A man with no hat, and with broken shoes, and with an old rag tied round his head. A man who had been soaked in water, and smothered in mud, and lamed by stones, and cut by flints, and stung by nettles, and torn by briars; who limped, and shivered, and glared and growled; and whose teeth chattered in his head as he seized me by the chin.

    "O! Don't cut my throat, sir," I pleaded in terror. "Pray don't do it, sir."

        Answer on p. 193

2. The first name mentioned in this passage is an enormous clue to the 2005 novel from which it comes.

Arthur believed, in a general way, that God existed, that boys were tempted by sin, and that the Fathers were right to beat them with the Tolley. When it came to particular articles of faith, he argued in private with his friend Partridge. Partridge liked to bamboozle a fellow, and not just on the cricket field.

"Are you aware that the doctrine of the Immaculate Conception became an article of faith as recently as 1854?"

"Somewhat late in the day, I'd have thought, Partridge?"

"Imagine. The Church has been debating the matter for centuries, and all that time it has never been heresy to deny the Virgin Birth. Now it is."

3. Quite a tricky mistake this one, so do feel free to guess.

Then felt I like some watcher of the skies
When a new planet swims into his ken;
Or like stout Cortez when with eagle eyes
He stared at the Pacific—and all his men
Looked at each other with a wild surmise—
Silent, upon a peak in Darien.

4. A phone call between London and Wall Street in one of the big American novels of the 1980s. The mistake won't be a very obvious one for American readers, so it might help to ask yourself what error an American author, even one so well-known for his assiduous research, might be most likely to make here.

The plastic speaker was the size of a bedside clock radio. Everyone stared at it, waiting for the voice of Gene Lopwitz. Lopwitz was in London where it was now 4:00 p.m. He would preside over this meeting by telephone.

"Yeah, I can hear you, Arnie. There was a lotta cheering going on."

"Where are you, Gene?" asked Arnold Parch.

"I'm at a cricket match." Then less clearly: "What's the name a this place again?" He was evidently with some other people. "Tottenham Park, Arnie. I'm on a kind of terrace."

"Who's playing?"

"Don't get technical on me, Arnie. A lot of very nice young gentlemen in cable-knit sweaters and white flannel pants, is the best I can tell you."

Appreciative laughter broke out in the room, and Sherman felt his own lips bending into the somehow obligatory smile.

Q7

Finally in this round, two where the mistakes should be easy enough for especially pedantic ornithologists to spot—but might need a little more guesswork from anybody else.

5. Be innocent of the knowledge, dearest chuck,
Till thou applaud the deed. Come, seeling night,
Scarf up the tender eye of pitiful day,
And with thy bloody and invisible hand
Cancel and tear to pieces that great bond
Which keeps me pale. Light thickens
And the crow makes wing to the rooky wood;
Good things of day begin to droop and drowse,

Answers on pp. 194–195

Whiles night's black agents to their preys do rouse.
Thou marvell'st at my words: but hold thee still.
Things bad begun make strong themselves by ill.
So, prithee, go with me.

6. This is from a commemorative poem by the British poet laureate of the day. The name of the poem isn't required, so people keeping score should get two points just for that laureate's name.

I'm glad that you are marrying at home
Below Sir Christopher's embracing dome;
Four-square on that his golden cross and ball
Complete our own cathedral of St. Paul.
Blackbirds in city churchyards hail the dawn,
Charles and Diana, on your wedding morn.

Round Three

Featured Author: Arthur Conan Doyle

1. Where was Doyle a medical student?

2. Which of Doyle's teachers at medical school was, significantly enough, a master of observation, logic, deduction, and diagnosis?

3. In the Holmes story "The Adventure of the Speckled Band," what's the speckled band?

4. What's unusual about the narrator of the Holmes story "The Adventure of the Blanched Soldier"?

5. Who narrates the story of the Giant Rat of Sumatra?

6. Many of the Holmes stories feature which Scotland Yard inspector?

7. What's the name of Holmes's older and even more brilliant brother?

8. In "The Adventure of the Final Problem," where does Holmes apparently die?

9. Name any of the three Doyle novels featuring Professor Challenger.

10. For the last ten years of his life, Doyle undertook a worldwide crusade for what?

Q7

Round Four

A Round on the Links: Literary Connections

Can you link the following literary people or things?

1. Margery Williams

   Mr. McGregor's enemy

   Roddy Doyle's first three novels (pronunciation-wise)

   Richard Adams

2. Dodie Smith's first novel—which still seems to be regarded by fans as her best

   The Robert Penn Warren novel that takes its title from a line in *Humpty-Dumpty*

   The first of the *Canterbury Tales*

   The eighteenth-century philosopher George Berkeley

3. The villainous Dartmoor resident Jack Stapleton, in 1902

   The first book by Charles Darwin

   The third novel by Frederick Forsyth, which takes its title from a line in *Julius Caesar*

   Robert B. Parker finishes off Raymond Chandler

Q7

4. (Linguistically speaking:)

Samuel Beckett

Vladimir Nabokov

Milan Kundera

John Milton

Answer on p. 202 186

Round Five

Oh, It's You Again: Literary Characters Who've Been in More than One Book

1. Which historical character features as a villain in Shakespeare's *Henry VI, Part One*—and has also been the main subject of a burlesque epic by Voltaire, a tragedy by Schiller, a long poem by Robert Southey, and dramas by Jean Anouilh and George Bernard Shaw?

2. In the Harry Potter novels, what are the four first names of Professor Dumbledore?

3. The 2007 novel *Michael Tolliver Lives* reintroduced the main character from which novel series, published between 1978 and 1990?

4. The police detective Steve Carella is the main character in whose 87th Precinct series of novels?

5. Which twelve-novel sequence is narrated by Nicholas Jenkins?

6. Who's the heroine of Emma Tennant's 1993 novel, *Pemberley*?

7. Who created Precious Ramotswe—Botswana's only female private detective?

8. Whose novels *Porno* and *Glue* featured some of the same characters as his first book, *Trainspotting*?

9. Dunstan Ramsay is a recurring character in many

of whose novels—including all three books in the Deptford trilogy?

10. Which long-running fictional character was named after the author of *A Field Guide to the Birds of the West Indies* (1936)?

Quiz Seven: Answers

Round One

Books and the Arts

1. Johannes Vermeer's

2. Bret Easton Ellis's

3. The Doors. Huxley's book was *The Doors of Perception*, which itself took its title from a line of William Blake's.

4. William Faulkner

5. John Osborne

6. Toni Morrison

7. She thinks Sickert was Jack the Ripper, as explained in her optimistically titled book *Portrait of a Killer: Jack the Ripper—Case Closed*

8. *Happy Days*. The play featured a woman buried in earth, and the sitcom featured the Fonz.

9. Thomas Pynchon, who made several gags about his reclusiveness. Later the same year, he "appeared" on the show again.

10. John Gay

Round Two

Pedants' Revolt: A Round of Literary Mistakes II

1. That was Pip meeting the convict Magwitch at the beginning of Charles Dickens's *Great Expectations*. But in Chapter 42, Magwitch reveals that he'd dived off a prison ship and swum to the shore: something that would have been impossible with a Victorian leg iron on. For a start, he'd never have surfaced after the dive—and even if he had, he couldn't have swum the hundreds of yards from where the ship would have been to the marshes. The simplest explanation for the error, as suggested by John Sutherland in one of his books of literary puzzles, is that Dickens, like most mid-Victorians, just didn't understand swimming—which wouldn't become a popular pastime until later in the century.

2. That was Julian Barnes from *Arthur and George*, in which the Arthur—seen there at Stonyhurst Jesuit School—is Arthur Conan Doyle, who is featured in Round Three. But, like many non-Catholics, Barnes has fallen into the trap of thinking that the Immaculate Conception is the same as the Virgin Birth. In fact, it's got nothing to do with the birth or conception of Jesus at all, but is the doctrine that his mother Mary was conceived without original sin. We also know that this was Barnes's mis-

take rather than Partridge's, because it was corrected for the paperback edition.

3. From "On First Looking into Chapman's Homer" by John Keats. Unfortunately, it wasn't Cortez—stout or otherwise—who was silent on a peak in Darien. Keats drew much of the poem's imagery from William Robertson's *History of America* (1777) and has confused two passages in the book: Cortez's entry into Mexico City, and Balboa's first sighting of the Pacific from the isthmus of Darien.

4. From *The Bonfire of the Vanities*, Tom Wolfe's classic novel of 1980s New York, whose main character, Sherman McCoy, is a Wall Street trader and what was known in those far-off days as a yuppie. However, Tottenham Park is not a London cricket ground of any kind, let alone one big enough to have terracing. It's actually a Jewish cemetery. (By the way, we earlier learned that the meeting is at 10 a.m. New York time, which means that it would be 3, not 4 p.m., in London.)

5. From Shakespeare's *Macbeth*, with Macbeth dropping dark hints to his wife about the forthcoming murder of Banquo. The Bard's mistake in that passage was pointed out a few years ago in an obsessively ornithological essay by John Crompton in the *Tennyson Research Bulletin*. Crompton started by denouncing Tennyson's bird-based howlers—including having a female nightingale singing—and broadened his attacks from there. Shakespeare's blunder leaves him especially aghast. "*Crows* do not make wing to the *rooky* wood," he writes

sternly. "The two species do not associate." His essay ends with the withering question: "Should A. S. Byatt have won the Booker Prize for *Possession* when she places flocks of ravens in Richmond Park?"

6. From Sir John Betjeman's poem on the royal wedding of July 1981. Sadly, as a Mr. K. H. Holdaker immediately explained in a letter to the *London Times*, Sir John had mistaken the yearly cycle of the common blackbird. "I fear not," wrote Mr. Holdaker about the chances of blackbirds hailing that particular dawn. "It is the moulting season. If you want blackbirds at the wedding, get married in spring."

A7

Round Three

Featured Author: Arthur Conan Doyle

1. Edinburgh University

2. Dr. Joseph Bell

3. A snake—to be precise, an Indian swamp adder

4. The narrator is Holmes himself. The only other story he narrates is "The Adventure of the Lion's Mane."

5. Nobody. This is one of the adventures we hear about in passing, but which is never told— apparently because, according to Holmes, it's "a story for which the world is not yet prepared."

6. Lestrade

7. Mycroft Holmes

8. The Reichenbach Falls in Switzerland. Famously, Doyle killed off Holmes so that he could concentrate on "more serious literary work." Even more famously, popular demand forced him to bring back Holmes a few years later. The ledge from which Holmes fell is now marked by a plaque in English, German, and French. The English inscription reads: "At this fearful place, Sherlock Holmes vanquished Professor Moriarty, on 4 May 1891."

9. *The Poison Belt*, *The Land of Mist*, and, best

A7

known these days, *The Lost World*—the one about dinosaurs.

10. Spiritualism. His *History of Spiritualism* was published in 1926, and *The Land of Mist* from the same year was a spiritualist novel. At the time, Doyle was by no means the only man of science who saw contacting the dead as the next great scientific challenge. The radio, the telephone, and the television were all invented partly because Guglielmo Marconi, Alexander Graham Bell, and John Logie Baird believed this, too—and thought their inventions might do the trick.

Round Four

A Round on the Links: Literary Connections

1. RABBITS (OR IN ONE CASE RABBITTES)

Margery Williams is the author of *The Velveteen Rabbit*, first published in 1922 and a children's favorite ever since. The book is subtitled *Or How Toys Become Real*, which apparently is by being loved. And if that's not cute enough for you, in 1984 there was a non-animated Disney version on television starring Marie Osmond as the rabbit.

Peter Rabbit survives a hair-raising chase after raiding Mr. McGregor's vegetables in *The Tale of Peter Rabbit* by Beatrix Potter. (Before the action of the book begins, Mr. McGregor has already killed Peter's father and put him in a pie.)

The Rabbitte family star in all of Roddy Doyle's first three novels: *The Commitments*, *The Snapper*, and *The Van*—now collectively called the Barrytown trilogy.

Richard Adams's first novel was the firmly rabbit-based *Watership Down*, rejected by at least twelve publishers before it became a worldwide bestseller and a hit film.

A7

Thanks to Disney, Dodie Smith may be most famous for *The Hundred and One Dalmatians*—but in the 1930s she'd been a successful playwright, before turning to fiction with *I Capture the Castle*, published when she was fifty-two. The book sold over a million copies, and its celebrity champions since have included Ralph Vaughan Williams, Joanna Trollope, and J. K. Rowling.

Warren's 1946 novel was *All the King's Men*, based on the life of Louisiana governor Huey Long, aka the Kingfish. The novel won the 1947 Pulitzer Prize for Fiction (or Pulitzer Prize for the Novel, as it was then called), and Warren is the only person ever to have won both that and the Pulitzer Prize for Poetry, which he did twice: in 1958 and 1979. And to continue the litany of triumph, the film of *All the King's Men* won the Oscar for Best Picture in 1949.

The first of Chaucer's *Canterbury Tales*, after the General Prologue, is "The Knight's Tale."

George Berkeley is more usually known as Bishop Berkeley, largely because he was the Bishop of Cloynes. Berkeley's idea that things exist only in that they are perceived led to the question: "If a tree falls in a forest and nobody is there to hear it, does it make a sound?" It also inspired a limerick by Monsignor Ronald Knox:

There was once a man who said, "God
Must think it exceedingly odd

200

    If he finds that this tree
    Continues to be
When there's no one about in the Quad."

This in turn inspired the anonymous reply:

Dear Sir, Your astonishment's odd:
I am always about in the Quad.
    And that's why the tree
    Will continue to be,
Since observed by Yours faithfully, God.

3. DOGS

Jack Stapleton is the baddie in *The Hound of the Baskervilles* by this quiz's featured author, Arthur Conan Doyle.

In 1839 Charles Darwin's first book was pithily titled *Journal of Researches into the Geology and Natural History of the Various Countries Visited by HMS Beagle*. Luckily it's published nowadays as simply *Voyage of the Beagle*.

Frederick Forsyth's third novel was *Dogs of War*, referring to mercenary soldiers, but also to Mark Antony's line: "Cry, 'Havoc!' and let slip the dogs of war."

When he died, Raymond Chandler left behind four short chapters of *Poodle Springs*, featuring a surprisingly married Philip Marlowe. (In Marlowe's defense, his wife, Linda Loring, did propose to him, rather than the other way around—at the end of Chandler's last completed novel *Playback*.) In 1988, on the centenary of Chandler's birth, his estate asked Robert B. Parker to complete the novel, which was published the following year.

4. THEY ALL WROTE IN MORE THAN ONE LANGUAGE

Beckett wrote in French and English, which explains why his play *En Attendant Godot* was performed two years before his play *Waiting for Godot*.

Nabokov was a successful Russian novelist before he became a successful American one. And as if that weren't impressive enough, he also made many important contributions to the study of butterflies and created several classic chess problems.

Perhaps best known for *The Unbearable Lightness of Being*, Kundera has written novels in both his native Czech and, more recently, in French—having left Communist Czechoslovakia for France in 1975.

From his teenage years onward, Milton produced poems in Latin and Italian, as well as in English.

Round Five

Oh, It's You Again: Literary Characters Who've Been in More than One Book

1. Joan of Arc

2. Albus Percival Wulfric Brian

3. The Tales of the City series by Armistead Maupin

4. Ed McBain's. (McBain was one of many pseudo-nyms used by Evan Hunter, who, for the record, was born Salvatore Lombino.)

5. *A Dance to the Music of Time* by Anthony Powell

6. Elizabeth Bennet. *Pemberley* is Tennant's sequel to *Pride and Prejudice*, taking its title from the name of Mr. Darcy's house in the original book. The sequel picked up the story a year after Elizabeth had married Mr. Darcy, and suggested the marriage wasn't going well. Tennant also wrote *Emma in Love*—in which Austen's heroine found some consolation for her unconsummated marriage to Mr. Knightley by having a lesbian affair. These novels have not, on the whole, gone down well with Austen fans.

7. Alexander McCall Smith

8. Irvine Welsh's

9. Robertson Davies's

10. James Bond. Ian Fleming, a keen bird-watcher, had

a copy of the book in his house in Jamaica—and took the name of its author, he later explained, because "I wanted the simplest, dullest, plainest-sounding name I could find. 'James Bond' was much better than something more interesting, like 'Peregrine Carruthers.'" In the film *Die Another Day*, Pierce Brosnan as Bond is seen reading *A Field Guide to the Birds of the West Indies* when he's in Cuba posing as an ornithologist.

Quiz Eight

Round One

A Literary Flowering: Books and Botany

(Note: The botany can come in either the questions or the answers.)

1. Whose first collection of poetry was *Leaves of Grass*?

2. Which British Nobel Prize winner's first novel was *The Grass Is Singing*?

3. In Kenneth Grahame's *Wind in the Willows*, the mole and the rat have a mystical vision of which god?

4. What was the first novel by David Guterson?

5. What was the first novel in James Ellroy's L.A. Quartet?

6. Who won the 1988 Pulitzer Prize for drama with *Driving Miss Daisy*?

7. Which long-running literary character is the protagonist of *The Mystery at Lilac Inn*, *The Message in the Hollow Oak*, and *The Phantom of Pine Hill*?

8. Who created the forensic sculptor Eve Duncan?

9. Which 1980s bestseller is set in an Italian monastery in 1327?

10. Whose novels include *Drawing Blood* and *Exquisite Corpse*?

Q8

Answers on p. 221

Round Two

Literary Feuds, Rivalries, and Rejections

1. From the diary of a writer sometimes thought of as a bit of a snob—which, given this entry, doesn't seem entirely unfair. Who's the writer and who, for a giveaway second point, is she writing about?

    16 August 1922
    I should be reading *Ulysses*, and fabricating my case for and against. I have read 200 pages so far—not a third; and have been amused, stimulated, charmed, interested, by the first 2 or 3 chapters; and then puzzled, bored, irritated and disillusioned by a queasy undergraduate scratching his pimples. An illiterate, underbred book it seems to me; the book of a self taught working man, and we all know how distressing they are, how egotistic, insistent; raw, striking; and ultimately nauseating.

Q8

2. From a 1991 volume of memoirs, complete with geographical clue. Again, writer and victim please, for one point each.

    While I was in Wales, I encountered the poet in the flesh. Apart from just one poem, "The Hunchback in the Park," which distinguishes itself from all the rest of his poetic output by not being about him, and a few isolated lines from other poems—'And death shall have no dominion," "Deep with the first dead lies London's daughter"—he strikes me as a very bad

Answers on p. 223

poet indeed, or else a brilliant one in a mode that is anathema to me. Either way he is a pernicious figure, one who has helped to get Wales and Welsh poetry a bad name and generally done lasting harm to both. The general picture he draws of the place and the people is false, sentimentalising, melodramatising, sensationalising, ingratiating.

3. Which American author is this, talking about a fist-fight with a fellow writer at a New York party held by Lally Weymouth? One point for that, and another for his opponent—who, given that you get his first name, shouldn't be too hard to identify. We pick up the story just as the speaker has felt a hand on his shoulder . . .

It was Norman, looking small, fat and out of shape. "You look like an old Jew," he said.
   "Well, Norman," I said in my witty way, "*you* look like an old Jew, too."
   Then he threw the contents of his glass in my face, and punched me gently on the side of the mouth. It didn't hurt. Then I pushed him. Norman has always hated the fact that, apart from anything else, I'm much taller and stronger than he is. He went flying backward six or seven feet, landing—to our alarm—on top of the man who invented Xerox.
   "Come outside," he said to me. His mouth was working and you could smell the fear. "Norman," I said, "you can't go *on* this way. You're too old for all this."

4. More of a legal than a physical fight now. This is from a book about an American novelist by the

British writer Ian Hamilton, and led to a lengthy courtroom wrangle. Who, for your two points, was Hamilton's subject?

Four years ago, I wrote to him, telling him that I proposed to write a study of his "life and work." Would he be prepared to answer a few questions? I could either visit him at his home in Cornish, New Hampshire, or I could put my really very elementary queries in the mail—which did he prefer?

All this was, of course, entirely disingenuous. I knew very well that he had been approached in this manner maybe a hundred times before, with no success. The idea of his "record" being straightened would, I was aware, be thoroughly repugnant to him. He didn't want there to *be* a record and—so far as I could tell—he was passionate in his contempt for the whole business of "literary biography."

5. One of the oddest publishers' rejections of the twentieth century, now. This is from the notes made by a reader for Alfred A. Knopf in New York in the summer of 1950. So, for two points, which book—which went on to become one of biggest nonfiction bestsellers of all time—did that reader somehow manage to describe like this?

Very dull. A dreary record of typical family bickering, petty annoyances, and adolescent emotions. Even if the work had come to light five years ago, when the subject was timely, I don't see that there would have been a chance for it.

211   Answers on p. 224

6. Finally in this round, a long-standing feud becomes the basis of a short story, where the first speaker here is telling the narrator about the alarming behavior of his brother-in-law. Who wrote the story—and who, fairly obviously, is the model for the brother-in-law? (Again, one point for each.)

"Do you know where Rodney is at this moment? Up in the nursery, bending over his son Timothy's cot, gathering material for a poem about the unfortunate little rat when asleep. Some baloney, no doubt, about how he hugs his teddy bear and dreams of angels. Yes, that is what he is doing, writing poetry about Timothy. Horrible whimsical stuff that . . . Well, when I tell you that he refers to him throughout as 'Timothy Bobbin,' you will appreciate what we are up against."

I am not a weak man, but I confess that I shuddered.

"Timothy Bobbin?"

"Timothy by golly Bobbin. No less."

Answer on pp. 224–225

Round Three

Featured Author: William Shakespeare

1. If Shakespeare's plays were arranged in alphabetical order by title, which one would come first?

2. What connects Shakespeare's mother with the setting of *As You Like It*?

3. Which stage direction explains the disappearance of Antigonus from *The Winter's Tale*?

4. What's the only Shakespeare play whose title contains an English place-name?

5. Which Shakespearean main character speaks the line: "Why, there they are both, baked in this pie"?

6. In *Romeo and Juliet*, is Romeo a Montague or a Capulet?

7. Between 1788 and 1820 why was *King Lear* not allowed to be performed in Britain?

8. Within a year either way, how old was Shakespeare when he got married?

9. In *Othello*, who kills Iago?

10. To the nearest thousand, how many direct descendants of Shakespeare are thought to be alive today?

   Answers on p. 227

Round Four

A Round on the Links: Literary Connections

Can you link the following literary people or things? (And this time, in honor of the featured author, the round is something of a Shakespeare special.)

1. Michel Faber's big 2002 bestseller about a Victorian prostitute

   The best-known literary creation by Baroness Orczy

   Anton Chekhov's dramatic orchard

   Cordelia's unsuccessful suitor in *King Lear*

2. *White Fang*

   The 1998 play by Michael Frayn featuring Niels Bohr and Werner Heisenberg talking quantum physics

   The twentieth-century philosopher whose 1978 essay collection *Russian Thinkers* included the highly influential "The Hedgehog and the Fox"?

   Juliet's unsuccessful suitor in *Romeo and Juliet*

3. Montmorency the Dog

   Luigi Pirandello

   Lord Peter Wimsey's tailors

   The Shakespeare play that's subtitled *What You Will*

4. The Woolfs' publishing firm

The fourth novel by the man whose first was *Digital Fortress*

Elbow in *Measure for Measure* . . .

. . . and the man whom Mark Twain believed wrote *Measure for Measure*

Answer on pp. 230–231

Round Five

Simply Seek Similar Sounds:
An Alliterative Round

All the answers here are literary people or things with alliterative names—and, in the usual helpful way of this book, over the course of the round the alliteration comes in alphabetical order.

1. Which 1,200-page book by Hervey Allen was the bestselling novel in America in 1933 and 1934?

2. In which 1968 novel by J. P. Donleavy is the main character in love with Miss Fitzdare?

3. What was the last novel by George Eliot?

4. Which German author won the 1999 Nobel Prize for Literature?

5. Which German-Swiss author, later a favorite of the hippies of the 1960s, wrote *Siddhartha* and *The Glass Bead Game*?

6. Who's the only alliterative eponymous main character in a novel by Charles Dickens?

7. What's the only poem now attributed to Chaucer's contemporary William Langland?

8. Which crime novelist has also written under the name Barbara Vine?

9. Which war poet also wrote an autobiographical

Answers on p. 233

trilogy of novels, published together in 1937 as *The Complete Memoirs of George Shearston*?

10. Who's the most famous literary creation of the Reverend Wilbert Awdry?

Answers on p. 233

Quiz Eight: Answers

Round One

A Literary Flowering: Books and Botany

1. Walt Whitman

2. Doris Lessing

3. Pan—in the chapter "The Piper at the Gates of Dawn," which also gave Pink Floyd the title of their first album

4. *Snow Falling on Cedars*

5. *Black Dahlia*. The other novels in the quartet are *The Big Nowhere*, *L.A. Confidential*, and *White Jazz*.

6. Alfred Uhry

7. Nancy Drew

8. Iris Johansen

9. *The Name of the Rose* by Umberto Eco

10. Poppy Z. Brite

A8

Round Two

Literary Feuds and Rivalries

1. Virginia Woolf ponders James Joyce and his recently published novel, *Ulysses*—although it was so rude that it couldn't be published anywhere but Paris. All these years later, Woolf is surely still the only reader of *Ulysses* to have found the book "illiterate."

2. Kingsley Amis giving Dylan Thomas a thorough kicking in the chapter from his *Memoirs* on his time in Swansea, South Wales. The kicking goes on for several pages, before Amis delivers the concise summary: "Dylan Thomas was an outstandingly unpleasant man, one who cheated and stole from his friends and peed on their carpets." It was also while he was in Swansea, lecturing in English at the university, that Amis published *Lucky Jim*. By the time of those *Memoirs* in 1991, the city had "again become what it was further back in my life: the piece of earth I know best, better than any part of London, and feel most at home in."

3. Gore Vidal speaking to the *London Sunday Telegraph* in 1977 about fighting Norman Mailer earlier the same year. The two men had famously clashed on a Dick Cavett TV show in 1971, but managed not to come to blows, although there were reports of Mailer head-butting Vidal afterward. As you might expect, Mailer's account of the

A8

fight was rather different from Vidal's. For one thing, he won.

4. That was the opening of Hamilton's *In Search of J. D. Salinger*. Salinger's celebrated reclusiveness dates back to at least 1961, when *Newsweek* had to illustrate an article about him with a photograph of his mailbox. Hamilton's original idea seems to have been to write a book about not being able to write a book about Salinger. Salinger, though, even blocked that in the courts. As a result, Hamilton ended up writing a book about not being able to write a book about not being able to write a book about Salinger.

5. That was the Knopf reader's verdict on *The Diary of Anne Frank*. Interesting, to say the least, that in 1950, the reader apparently felt the Holocaust was old news—while the phrase "petty annoyances" does seem especially harsh as a description of hiding from the Nazis. The diary was eventually published in America by Doubleday under the title *Anne Frank: Diary of a Young Girl* and has now sold around 30 million copies worldwide.

6. That was P. G. Wodehouse in a story called "Rodney Has a Relapse"—where the poet Rodney Spelvin becomes a chance for Wodehouse to have a vigorous swipe at A. A. Milne. Presumably, Wodehouse was being so uncharacteristically vicious because in 1941, when he made a series of controversial broadcasts from Germany, where he was a prisoner of war, Milne had been one of his severest critics. (After the war, Wodehouse never

lived in England again, becoming an American citizen in 1955.) And just to make sure we don't miss the point, Wodehouse also gives us some of Spelvin's Timothy Bobbin poems—one of which goes like this:

> Timothy Bobbin has ten little toes.
> He takes them out walking wherever he goes.
> And if Timothy gets a cold in the head,
> His ten little toes stay with him in bed.

In the story, the brother-in-law also goes on to say that Rodney "is laying up a lifetime of shame and misery for the wretched little moppet"—which is certainly what happened in Christopher Robin's case. The adult Christopher Milne once described his dad's poem "Vespers" (the one about Christopher Robin saying his prayers) as "a toe-curling, fist-clenching, lip-biting" source of embarrassment.

A8

Round Three

Featured Author: William Shakespeare

1. *All's Well That Ends Well*

2. The word "Arden." Shakespeare's mother's maiden name was Mary Arden, and the setting of *As You Like It* is the Forest of Arden.

3. "Exit, pursued by a bear"

4. *The Merry Wives of Windsor*

5. Titus Andronicus—explaining to Tamora the whereabouts of her two sons, whom he's slaughtered and put in the pie she's just been eating

6. A Montague

7. Because it portrayed a fictional mad king at a time when Britain had a real mad king in George III

8. Eighteen—when Anne Hathaway, his bride, was twenty-six and pregnant. In *Twelfth Night*, Orsino gives the apparently heartfelt advice that a husband should always be older than his wife.

9. A slight trick question, this one. The answer is nobody. Iago is still alive at the end of the play, although he is about to be dragged off and tortured.

10. Another slight trick question. The answer is none— his last grandchild, Elizabeth Hall, died childless in 1670.

Round Four

A Round on the Links: Literary Connections

1. SHADES OF RED

Michel Faber's nine-hundred-page bestseller was
The Crimson Petal and the White.

Baroness Orczy created the Scarlet Pimpernel—
definitely better known than her later creation, the
aristocratic female detective, Lady Molly of
Scotland Yard.

The Cherry Orchard was Chekhov's last play, about
the decline of an aristocratic family, who are forced
to sell their estate, and leave at the end to the sound
of their beloved orchard being chopped down. The
play also shows the soulnessness of the rising middle
class. Chekhov considered it a comedy.

The Duke of Burgundy asks for Cordelia's hand in
the first scene of Shakespeare's *King Lear*—but loses
out to the King of France, mainly because he won't
take her without a dowry.

2. CAPITAL CITIES

White Fang, the 1906 tale of a dog in the Klondike
gold rush, is by Jack London.

The Michael Frayn play is *Copenhagen*—based on
Bohr and Heisenberg's meeting there in 1941.

A8

Russian Thinkers was by Isaiah <u>Berlin</u>. In the program for the New York production of his trilogy *The Coast of Utopia* in 2006, Tom Stoppard mentioned how much Berlin's book had influenced the plays—which, much to the publishers' surprise, led to it suddenly being in hot demand.

Count <u>Paris</u> is Juliet's suitor and the man her parents want her to marry in Shakespeare's play—before she falls for Romeo instead.

3. THE THREE TIMES TABLE

Montmorency is from *<u>Three</u> Men in a Boat* by Jerome K. Jerome, and even makes it into the subtitle: *To Say Nothing of the Dog!*

Pirandello was the Italian avant-garde author and dramatist who won the Nobel Prize for Literature in 1934—and whose most performed play is *<u>Six</u> Characters in Search of an Author*.

The <u>Nine</u> Tailors is one of the Lord Peter Wimsey novels by Dorothy L. Sayers, with the title referring to a pattern of bell-ringing.

What You Will is the subtitle of *<u>Twelfth</u> Night*.

4. THE NAMES OF ARTISTS

Virginia Woolf and husband, Leonard, founded the <u>Hogarth</u> Press. This was named after Hogarth House, where they were living at the time, and became an early publisher of T. S. Eliot, along with translations of Tolstoy and Chekhov.

Digital Fortress was the first novel by Dan Brown—and his fourth was *The Da Vinci Code*, so successful that *Digital Fortress* and his other books were soon reissued and became bestsellers, too.

Elbow in *Measure for Measure* is a <u>constable</u>—for our purposes, as in John.

In his book *Is Shakespeare Dead?* Mark Twain was another of the distinguished men of his day to go along with the theory that Shakespeare's plays were written by <u>Francis Bacon</u>—also the name of a twentieth-century British painter. To be scrupulously accurate, what Twain said was: "I only *believed* Bacon wrote Shakespeare, whereas I *knew* Shakespeare didn't."

A8

Round Five

Simply Seek Similar Sounds:
An Alliterative Round

1. *Anthony Adverse*

2. *The Beastly Beatitudes of Balthasar B*—which clearly had to feature in this round somewhere. Donleavy's other books include *The Saddest Summer of Samuel S, The Destinies of Darcy Dancer, Gentleman*—and, on a less alliterative note, *A Fairy Tale of New York*, which gave the Pogues the title of their most famous song.

3. *Daniel Deronda*

4. Gunter Grass—perhaps most famous for *The Tin Drum* and, these days, for his possible Nazi past

5. Herman Hesse—also a Nobel Prize winner in 1946

6. Nicholas Nickleby

7. *Piers Plowman*—which, suitably for this round, was a product of the medieval Alliterative Revival

8. Ruth Rendell

9. Siegfried Sassoon. The novels were *Memoirs of a Fox-Hunting Man, Memoirs of an Infantry Officer,* and *Shearston's Progress.*

10. *Thomas the Tank Engine*

A8

Quiz Nine

Round One

The Five Senses

1. Who created the famously deaf Quasimodo, the hunchback of Notre-Dame?

2. Who created the famously smelly Fungus the Bogeyman?

3. Who wrote the 1985 novel *Perfume*?

4. *Touching the Void* was a nonfiction bestseller by whom?

5. Which then-teenager wrote the play *A Taste of Honey*?

6. Which novel by Ford Madox Ford begins, "This is the saddest story I have ever heard."

7. Which E. M. Forster novel contains a celebrated tribute to Beethoven's Fifth Symphony?

8. Who won the National Book Award for Fiction in 1985 with *White Noise*?

Q9

9. In which novel would you find blind Pew?

10. Who wrote this two-line poem?

> Men seldom make passes
> At girls who wear glasses.

  Answers on p. 249

Round Two

What Happened Next?

This round features extracts that immediately precede lines of prose or poetry that are now very famous indeed. Your challenge, as you might imagine, is to identify what entry in every dictionary of quotations ever since is about to come next. (In the case of the poetry, of course, the rhyme scheme should help.) A big four if you can do this just from the extract itself. The normal two points if you need the name of the author and work first—and these can all be found at the back of the book on page 288.

1. In the Spring a fuller crimson comes upon the robin's breast;
   In the Spring the wanton lapwing gets himself another crest;
   In the Spring a livelier iris changes on the burnish'd dove . . .

2. Anything approaching the change that came over his features I have never seen before, and hope never to see again. Oh, I wasn't touched. I was fascinated. It was as though a veil had been rent. I saw on that ivory face the expression of sombre pride, of ruthless power, of craven terror—of an intense and hopeless despair. Did he live his life again in every detail of desire, temptation, and surrender during that supreme moment of complete knowledge? He cried in a whisper at some image, at some vision—he

Q9

Answers on p. 251

cried out twice, a cry that was no more than a
breath . . .

3. No Place so Sacred from such Fops is barr'd,
   Nor is Paul's Church more safe than Paul's
       Churchyard:
   Nay, fly to Altars; there they'll talk you dead;
   For . . .

4. No man is an island, entire of itself; every man is a
   piece of the continent, a part of the main. If a clod
   be washed away by the sea, Europe is the less, as
   well as if a promontory were; any man's death dimin-
   ishes me, because I am involved in mankind; and
   therefore never send to know . . .

5. If you can dream—and not make dreams your master
   If you can think—and not make thoughts your aim . . .

6. A slightly trickier rhyme scheme here, but it still
   should help.

   The year's at the spring
   And day's at the morn;
   Morning's at seven;
       The hillside's dew-pearled;
   The lark's on the wing;
   The snail's on the thorn . . .

Answers on pp. 251–252   240

Round Three

Featured Author: Agatha Christie

1. What's the name of Miss Marple's village?

2. What kind of novels did Christie publish under the pseudonym of Mary Westmacott?

3. In what context did Christie use the pseudonym of Teresa Neele?

4. *The Mousetrap* opened in London in 1952. Within three years either way, in which year did it become the longest-running play in British theatrical history?

5. Who connects the first London production of *The Mousetrap* with Gandhi and Steve Biko?

6. Within two inches either way, how tall was Hercule Poirot?

7. What was the profession of Christie's second husband, Max Mallowan?

8. Who once called Hercule Poirot "a detestable, bombastic, tiresome, egocentric little creep"?

9. Where did Christie get the title for her 1961 novel *The Pale Horse*?

10. According to *The Guinness Book of World Records*, how many novelists in literary history have sold more books than Agatha Christie?

Q9

Round Four

A Round on the Links: Literary Connections

Can you link the following literary people or things?

1. William Sydney Porter (by the sound of it)

   Larry McMurtry in 1985

   Alexandre Dumas in 1844

   How the eternal footman laughs at J. Alfred Prufrock

2. (These come in the right order.)

   Laurie Lee's 1969 follow-up to *Cider with Rosie*

   Arthur Koestler's 1940 attack on Stalinism

   Forks, Washington

   Mark Haddon's bestselling novel, narrated by an autistic child

A couple more of the purely factual ones now. This time, the link in each case is between four novels—although you do sometimes have to work out what those novels are . . .

3. Jay McInerney's *Bright Lights, Big City*

   Graham Greene's novel about a priest on the run in the Mexican revolution

   Henry James's *Turn of the Screw*

   Sinister goings-on at Manderley

4. The 1847 novel narrated by Lockwood and Nelly Dean

The Bell Jar

Scarlett O'Hara living in Tara

Savrola by Winston Churchill

Answer on pp. 257–258

Round Five

Body of Literature: A Biological Round

All the answers here contain or comprise a part of the human body.

1. Which novel of 2000 begins with Archie Jones attempting suicide on Cricklewood Broadway in London?

2. In which bestseller of 1974 are the main (human) characters Martin Brody, Matt Hooper, and Quint?

3. What's the first phrase of Virgil's *Aeneid*? (In English will do.)

4. What's the first word—and indeed, the second, third, fourth, and fifth words—of Tom Stoppard's *Rosencrantz and Guildenstern Are Dead*?

5. What's the title of Christy Brown's autobiography?

6. What was Alice Sebold's bestselling debut novel?

7. What was the first novel by Flannery O'Connor?

8. What line of dialogue follows this stage direction in Christopher Marlowe's play *Dr. Faustus*: "Enter Helen again, passing over between two cupids"?

9. Sue Trinder is the main character in which Sarah Waters novel?

10. In which African American classic is the main character called Janie Crawford?

Q9

Answers on p. 259

Quiz Nine: Answers

Round One

The Five Senses

1. Victor Hugo—in *Notre-Dame de Paris*

2. Raymond Briggs

3. Patrick Süskind

4. Joe Simpson

5. Shelagh Delaney

6. *The Good Soldier*

7. *Howards End*, where Forster calls the symphony "the most sublime noise that has ever penetrated into the ear of man"

8. Don DeLillo

9. *Treasure Island* by Robert Louis Stevenson

10. Dorothy Parker. The poem is called "News Item."

A9

Round Two

What Happened Next?

1. "In the Spring a young man's fancy lightly turns to thoughts of love."

   There's a nice (and surely accurate) parody of Tennyson's sentiments by E. Y. Harburg, the man who wrote "Over the Rainbow":

   > In the Spring a young man's fancy lightly turns
   >   to thoughts of love;
   > And in summer,
   > And in autumn,
   > And in winter—
   > See above.

2. "The horror! The horror!" The dying words of Mr. Kurtz, which possibly became even more famous when spoken by Marlon Brando in *Apocalypse Now*, when the film updated Conrad's story to the Vietnam War.

   A9

3. "Fools rush in where Angels fear to tread"—one of the few lines of eighteenth-century poetry to feature in songs by both Frank Sinatra and Elvis Presley, as well as the title of an E. M. Forster novel. Nor is it the only phrase from "An Essay on Criticism" that's entered the language. The poem also contains: "To err is human, to forgive, divine," "A little learning is a dangerous thing,"

and "What oft was thought but ne'er so well expressed." Pope was twenty-one when he wrote it.

4. ". . . for whom the bells tolls; it tolls for thee."

5. "If you can meet with Triumph and Disaster / And treat those two impostors just the same"

6. "God's in His heaven—
   All's right with the world!"

On a less lovely note, "Pippa Passes" has also become notorious for containing the word "twats"—which, though Browning didn't realize it, has always had the same meaning as it does today. The story goes that when the editors of the *Oxford English Dictionary* wrote to ask what he meant by it, Browning replied that it was a piece of headgear for nuns. He knew this because he'd once read a poem published in 1659 called "Vanity of Vanities," which attacked an overambitious priest with the lines:

They talk't of his having a Cardinall's Hat;
They'd send him as soon an Old Nun's Twat.

Round Three

Featured Author: Agatha Christie

1. St. Mary Mead

2. Romances. The fact that Christie and Westmacott were one and the same remained a secret for the first four of the six Westmacott novels—until the *London Sunday Times* revealed all in 1949.

3. During her mysterious disappearance in 1926, when she apparently suffered a nervous breakdown. The discovery of her abandoned car led to intense media speculation in Britain and national appeals for information. Christie was eventually found nearly two weeks later staying in a provincial hotel under the name Mrs. Teresa Neele—which also seems to have been the name of her then-husband's mistress. Perhaps not surprisingly, the incident went unmentioned in her autobiography.

4. 1958—and forty-four years later it was still going strong enough for the queen to attend the fiftieth anniversary Royal Gala Performance. (In Canada, mind you, the play did less well: opening in 1977 and closing after just twenty-six and a half years.) Back in 1952, Christie had signed over any royalties the play might earn to her seven-year-old grandson as a little gift.

5. Richard Attenborough—who was in the original

A9

cast and went on to direct films about Gandhi
(*Gandhi*) and Biko (*Cry Freedom*)

6. Five foot, four inches—according to Christie's first
   book, *The Mysterious Affair at Styles*

7. He was an archaeologist, specializing in Iraq and
   Syria

8. Agatha Christie—in 1960 during one of her many
   periods of being a bit sick of her best-loved creation. As early as 1938 she'd made the slightly gen-
   tler point, "There are moments when I have felt:
   'Why—why—why did I ever invent this detestable,
   bombastic, tiresome little man?'"

9. From the Book of Revelation in the Bible, where
   death rides a pale horse

10. None

Round Four

A Round on the Links: Literary Connections

1. CHOCOLATE

William Sydney Porter was the real name of
O. Henry, the short-story writer who specialized in
those sudden twists at the end. It's sometimes suggested that the <u>Oh Henry!</u> candy bar was named for
him, but sadly there's no evidence for this.

Larry McMurtry's *Lonesome <u>Dove</u>* was published
in 1985, winning the Pulitzer Prize the following
year and becoming a TV miniseries in 1989.
McMurtry's previous novel *Desert Rose*—set in Las
Vegas—carried the strange dedication: "To Lesley,
for the use of her goat."

Alexandre Dumas's 1844 novel was *The <u>Three
Musketeers</u>*—which, along with *The Count of Monte
Cristo*, made him one of the bestselling French
writers of the nineteenth century. In 2002, Dumas's
body was exhumed from a cemetery in northern
France and carried in a televised procession to the
Panthéon in Paris, to be laid alongside the likes of
Voltaire, Rousseau, Victor Hugo, Émile Zola, Marie
Curie, and Louis Braille. His coffin was draped in a
blue flag carrying the musketeers' motto ("All for
one, one for all") and was carried by Republican
Guards dressed as the three musketeers—Athos,
Porthos, and Aramis—and their leader, D'Artagnan.

A9

In T. S. Eliot's *Love Song of J. Alfred Prufrock*, Prufrock says, "I have seen the eternal footman hold my coat and snicker." The footman in question therefore <u>snickers</u>.

2. TIMES OF THE DAY

Lee's *As I Walked Out One Midsummer <u>Morning</u>*, the second volume of his autobiography, takes him from Gloucestershire via London and on to Spain, then on the eve of civil war.

Koestler had himself been a Communist, but left the party in 1938 because of Stalin's show trials, which form the basis of his novel *Darkness at <u>Noon</u>*. Koestler's later interests included LSD, Eastern religion, and euthanasia. In 1983, suffering from Parkinson's disease and leukemia, he committed suicide, along with his wife, leaving a will that endowed a chair of parapsychology at the University of Edinburgh. Among his fans is Sting, who named the Police album *The Ghost in the Machine* after a Koestler book.

Forks, Washington, is the setting for the <u>Twilight</u> series of books by Stephenie Meyer—and now it is a tourist attraction for her fans.

Mark Haddon's bestseller was 2003's *Curious Incident of the Dog in the <u>Night-Time</u>*, a title taken from a line in the Sherlock Holmes story "The Adventure of the Silver Blaze." Because Christopher, the fifteen-year-old narrator, is fascinated by prime numbers, the novel begins with Chapter 2, and ends fifty-one chapters later with Chapter 233.

3. NOVELS WITH UNNAMED MAIN CHARACTERS

Bright Lights, Big City is written in the second person—as in "You are at a nightclub talking to a girl with a shaved head"—so we never learn the name of the party-going, coke-snorting protagonist in 1980s Manhattan. Nor do we ever find out the name of the whisky priest in Greene's *Power and the Glory*. Nor of the governess who narrates the ghostly goings-on with her charges Miles and Flora in *The Turn of the Screw*. Nor of the narrator of Daphne du Maurier's *Rebecca* who has such a hard time at Manderley as the second Mrs. de Winter—Rebecca being the first.

4. THE ONLY NOVELS THEIR AUTHORS WROTE

Lockwood and Nelly Dean between them narrate *Wuthering Heights*, the only novel by Emily Brontë, who was thirty when she died in 1848.

The Bell Jar, Sylvia Plath's only novel, was published in Britain in 1963, a month before she died—also aged thirty. Because of its autobiographical candor, complete with frank descriptions of depression and mental hospitals, the book came out in England under the pseudonym Victoria Lucas. It wasn't published at all in America until 1971, because her mother feared it would embarrass Plath's friends, several of whom appear in thinly disguised form. (The family mightn't have been best pleased either.)

Scarlett O'Hara is the heroine of *Gone With the Wind*, the only novel by Margaret Mitchell.

A9

(Despite the claims of the publishers when it came out in 1996, a short story she'd written when she was sixteen doesn't count.) In 1949, thirteen years after its publication, Mitchell was knocked down and killed by a car in Atlanta. Even before the 1939 film the book was already a big bestseller. It went on to become one of the biggest of the century.

In 1953 Churchill won the Nobel Prize for Literature for his historical works. His only novel, *Savrola*, had been published in 1900 and was a political/adventure tale set in the fictional country of Laurania.

And if *To Kill a Mockingbird* hadn't already been used for another connections question, it could also have been in this one. Published in 1960, it became another of the twentieth century's biggest bestsellers—yet Harper Lee (who's still alive as of 2009) hasn't written so much as a paragraph of fiction since.

Round Five

Body of Literature: A Biological Round

1. *White Teeth* by Zadie Smith

2. *Jaws* by Peter Benchley. After the colossal success of the book, Peter Benchley tried for a while to show there was more to him than sharks—partly by writing *The Beast*, which was about a giant squid. His later books, though, included *Shark Trouble, White Shark, Shark Life,* and *Shark!*

3. "I sing of arms and the man." (In Latin, the phrase is *"Arma virumque cano."*

4. "Heads"—the two main characters are playing a coin-tossing game where the coin keeps coming down heads

5. *My Left Foot*

6. *The Lovely Bones*

7. *Wise Blood*

8. "Was this the face that launched a thousand ships?" (The Helen in that stage direction is Helen of Troy, whom Faustus has gotten the devil to conjure up after selling his soul.)

9. *Fingersmith*

10. *Their Eyes Were Watching God* by Zora Neale Hurston

A9

Quiz Ten

Round One

Books and Buildings

1. Which literary building is owned by the Earls of Groan?

2. In A. A. Milne's book of that name, who lives in the house at Pooh Corner?

3. Who wrote the novel *The House of the Seven Gables*?

4. Who drew on her American-frontier childhood for the Little House on the Prairie series?

5. Whose first novel was *Behind the Scenes at the Museum*?

6. Whose fourth novel was *Hotel du Lac*?

7. In which literary work would you find Doubting Castle?

8. Which poet's second collection was *Lord Weary's Castle*—which includes one of his best-known poems, "The Quaker Graveyard in Nantucket"?

9. Who wrote the novella *The Ballad of the Sad Café*?

10. In Roald Dahl's *James and the Giant Peach*, where does the peach finally come to rest?

 Answers on p. 277

Round Two

Did *You* Get That Far? Last Lines
That Maybe Not Everybody Reaches

Fittingly enough, the final extracts round features the final sentences of some very famous books. The twist is that they're also the sort of books that not all readers will necessarily have made it to the final sentences of. Using your skill, judgment, and perhaps even knowledge, can you identify the book and author in each case?

1. A novel of the 1860s:

    Just as in astronomy the difficulty of admitting the motion of the earth lay in the immediate sensation of the earth's stationariness, so in history the difficulty of recognising the subjection of the personality to the laws of space and time and causation lies in the difficulty of surmounting the direct sensation of the independence of one's personality.
    In the first case, we had to surmount the sensation of an unreal immobility in space, and to admit a motion we could not perceive of by sense. In the present case, it is as essential to surmount a consciousness of an unreal freedom and to recognise a dependence not perceived by our senses.

Q10

2. A nonfiction book of 1988:

    If we do discover a complete theory, it should in time be understandable in broad principle by everyone, not just a few scientists. Then we shall all, philoscphers, scientists, and just ordinary people, be able to take part in the discussion of the question of why it is that we and the universe exist. If we find the answer to that, it would be the ultimate triumph of human reason—for then we would know the mind of God.

3. A seventeenth-century novel:

I shall be proud and satisfied to have been the first author to enjoy the full effect of his own writing. For my sole object has been to arouse men's contempt for the all fabulous and absurd stories of knight errantry, whose credit this tale has already shaken, and which will, without a doubt, soon tumble to the ground. Farewell.

4. A work of history completed in 1787:

The historian may applaud the importance and variety of his subject; but, while he is conscious of his own imperfections, he must often accuse the deficiency of his materials. It was among the ruins of the Capitol, that I first conceived the idea of a work which has amused and exercised near twenty years of my life, and which, however inadequate to my own wishes, I finally deliver to the curiosity and candour of the Public.

5. A biography of 1791:

When there was an audience, his real opinions could seldom be gathered from his talk; though when he was in company with a single friend, he

Answers on p. 279–280

would discuss a subject with genuine fairness; but he was too conscientious to make an error permanent and pernicious, by deliberately writing it; and in all his numerous works, he earnestly inculcated what appeared to him to be the truth; his piety being constant, and the ruling principle of all his conduct.

Such was – –, a man whose talents, acquirements, and virtues were so extraordinary, that the more his character is considered, the more he will be regarded by the present age, and by posterity, with admiration and reverence.

6. A novel of the early twentieth century (and the last word of this punishingly long closing sentence is probably the biggest clue):

But at least, if strength were granted me for long enough to accomplish my work, I should not fail, even if the results were to make them resemble monsters, to describe men first and foremost as occupying a place, a very considerable place compared with the restricted one which is allotted to them in space, a place on the contrary prolonged past measure—for simultaneously, like giants plunged into the years, they touch epochs that are immensely far apart, separated by the slow accretion of many, many days—in the dimension of Time.

Q10

Round Three

Featured Author: Charles Dickens

1. In *Oliver Twist*, as whom is John Dawkins better known?

2. Which of his novels did Dickens say was his own favorite?

3. Dickens's fourth novel was the first he'd published not to have the main character's name in the title. What was it?

4. In *A Christmas Carol*, who's Tiny Tim's father?

5. What are the first twelve words of *A Tale of Two Cities*?

6. (Quite a hard one admittedly.) Which Dickens novel has a plot that centers on someone leaving money to his nephew's lover's guardian's brother's youngest daughter?

7. In which Dickens novel would you find the characters Mr. Chadband, Mr. Snagsby, Mrs. Jellyby, and Mr. Turveydrop?

8. Complete this piece of Dickens criticism by Oscar Wilde: "One must have a heart of stone to read the death of Little Nell . . ."

9. What novel did Dickens leave unfinished at the time of his death?

Q10

10. When Dickens died was he fifty-eight, sixty-eight, or seventy-eight?

Answer on p. 281

Round Four

A Round on the Links: Literary Connections

Can you link the following literary people or things?

1. *No Safe Place, Eyes of a Child, Dark Lady*

   A Cool Million, Miss Lonelyhearts, The Day of the Locust

   John Steinbeck provides a hit movie for James Dean

   James A. Michener provides a hit musical for Rodgers and Hammerstein

2. Henry Perowne, neurosurgeon

   The late Jack Dodds, Bermondsey butcher

   Leopold Bloom

   Clarissa Dalloway

3. *Flowers in the Attic*

   A Streetcar Named Desire

   "Rip Van Winkle"

   Louise Rennison's confessions of a teenage girl

Q10

4. (Finally, and appropriately:)

   Giles Foden's first novel

 Answers on pp. 283–286

Nikos Kazantzakis controversially fictionalizes the life of Jesus

Uncas in a novel of 1826

Plato tells of the death of his mentor

Round Five

And Finally: Literary Lasts, Conclusions, and Farewells

1. Who wrote the autobiographical novel *Goodbye to Berlin*?

2. Who wrote the controversial novel *Last Exit to Brooklyn*?

3. Which historian made his name in 1947 with *The Last Days of Hitler*?

4. Who wrote the much-anthologized poem "My Last Duchess"?

5. What's the last novel in Philip Pullman's His Dark Materials trilogy?

6. What's the last (and Booker-winning) novel in Pat Barker's Regeneration trilogy?

7. Who won the 1988 PEN/Faulkner award for *World's End*?

8. Which poem ends with these lines?

   A sadder and a wiser man,
   He rose the morrow morn.

Q10

9. Whose autobiographical novels of gay life include 1997's *Farewell Symphony*?

10. What are the last four words spoken by Hamlet?

Quiz Ten: Answers

Round One

Books and Buildings

1. Gormenghast, in the books by Mervyn Peake

2. Eeyore

3. Nathaniel Hawthorne

4. Laura Ingalls Wilder. *Little House on the Prairie* itself was the second in the series—and much debate still rages as to whether the books, written in the third person, are straight autobiography or autobiographical fiction.

5. Kate Atkinson

6. Anita Brookner

7. *The Pilgrim's Progress* by John Bunyan

8. Robert Lowell

9. Carson McCullers—who rather specialized in striking titles. Her novels include *The Heart Is a Lonely Hunter* and *Reflections in a Golden Eye*. She also wrote a play called *The Square Root of Wonderful* and a collection of poems called *Sweet as a Pickle and Clean as a Pig*.

10. On top of the Empire State Building

A10

Round Two

Did *You* Get That Far? Last Lines
That Maybe Not Everybody Reaches

1. Leo Tolstoy pondering the nature of history, and
   free will versus determinism, in the less-than-
   punchy final sentences of *War and Peace*—possibly
   the daddy of them all when it comes to not-always-
   read bestsellers. Still, you could always follow the
   example of Woody Allen, who once explained that:
   "I took a speed-reading course and read *War and
   Peace* in twenty minutes. It's about Russia."

2. The rousing finale to Stephen Hawking's *A Brief
   History of Time*, which spent a record 237 weeks
   on the *London Sunday Times* bestseller lists. One
   reason for its success may have been that Hawking
   reluctantly followed the advice he was given that
   "each equation I included in the book would halve
   the sales." In the end, he put in only one: $E=mc^2$.

3. The closing words of *Don Quixote* by Miguel de
   Cervantes. According to Martin Amis, "While
   clearly an impregnable masterpiece, *Don Quixote*
   suffers from one fairly serious flaw—that of
   outright unreadability. The book bristles with
   beauties, charm, sublime comedy; it is also, for
   long stretches (approaching about 75 percent of
   the whole), inhumanly dull."

4. Edward Gibbon reaching the end of *The History of
   the Decline and Fall of the Roman Empire*. In that

A10

279

passage you can almost hear his sigh of relief—but he later wrote, rather poignantly, that his initial sense of freedom at finishing the book was followed by a feeling of melancholy at taking "an everlasting leave of an old and agreeable companion."

5. James Boswell paying a final tribute to his subject and friend in *The Life of Samuel Johnson*. Just in case you're wondering, Johnson's opinions couldn't be trusted when there was an audience, because "from a spirit of contradiction, and a delight in showing his powers, he would often maintain the wrong side with equal warmth and ingenuity."

6. The end of the final volume of Marcel Proust's *À la recherche du temps perdu*—which means that sentence comes on page 3,294 of the three-volume Penguin UK edition.

Round Three

Featured Author: Charles Dickens

1. The Artful Dodger

2. *David Copperfield.* The year before his death, Dickens wrote a preface to the novel which contained this touching admission: "Of all my books, I like this the best. I am a fond parent to every child of my fancy . . . But, like many fond parents, I have in my heart of hearts a favorite child. And his name is *David Copperfield.*"

3. *The Old Curiosity Shop*—the first three being *The Pickwick Papers*, *Oliver Twist*, and *Nicholas Nickleby*

4. Bob Cratchit

5. "It was the best of times, it was the worst of times."

6. *Little Dorrit.* (To be strictly ethical, it should be acknowledged that this description of the plot comes from *The Information* by Martin Amis.)

7. *Bleak House*

8. ". . . without laughing."

9. *The Mystery of Edwin Drood*

10. Fifty-eight

A10

Round Four

A Round on the Links: Literary Connections

1. POINTS OF THE COMPASS

No Safe Place, Eyes of a Child, and *Dark Lady* are three of the bestsellers by Richard <u>North</u> Patterson.

A Cool Million, Miss Lonelyhearts, and *The Day of the Locust* are three of the four novellas by Nathanael <u>West</u>, who was killed in a car crash at age thirty-seven, on December 22, 1940—the day after his friend (and fellow Hollywood screenwriter) F. Scott Fitzgerald died of a heart attack. For modern readers, one of the most striking aspects of *The Day of the Locust* is that it features a character named Homer Simpson.

James Dean's first major screen role was in *<u>East</u> of Eden,* based on the novel Steinbeck considered to be his best.

Michener's first work, *Tales from the <u>South</u> Pacific,* was a collection of short stories that drew on his own experiences in the navy during World War II. For the musical *South Pacific,* Rodgers and Hammerstein turned the stories into a single narrative.

A10

2. THE MAIN CHARACTERS OF NOVELS WHOSE ACTION LASTS FOR ONE DAY

Henry Perowne is the protagonist of *Saturday*—Ian

283

McEwan's novel set on Saturday, February 15, 2003, the day of the demonstrations in London against the Iraq war.

Jack Dodds is—sort of—the main character of *Last Orders* by Graham Swift, because his are the ashes being carried to Margate by his friends on the day the novel describes.

Leopold Bloom is in James Joyce's *Ulysses*, set in Dublin on June 16, 1904, the day Joyce had had his first date with his future lover and eventual wife, Nora Barnacle. (The book's publication date was personally significant, too: February 2, 1922, was Joyce's fortieth birthday.)

Clarissa Dalloway is the heroine of Virginia Woolf's *Mrs. Dalloway*, which follows her through a day on which she's hosting a party.

3 · PEOPLE WITH THE SAME FIRST NAMES AS AMERICAN STATES

Flowers in the Attic is the 1979 bestseller by <u>Virginia</u> Andrews. She later became so successful that after she died in 1986 her estate hired a ghost writer to continue producing books in her name.

<u>Tennessee</u> Williams's *Streetcar Named Desire* is the play featuring faded Southern belle Blanche DuBois having a rough time in New Orleans—until she's led off to a mental hospital with her farewell line: "I have always depended on the kindness of strangers."

"Rip Van Winkle" is the story by <u>Washington</u>

Irving, about a man in New York's Catskill mountains who falls asleep for twenty years. When he wakes up, he discovers that the American Revolution has taken place. He also discovers that his nagging wife is dead—which makes some of the village's other henpecked husbands wish they'd been so lucky.

Confessions of <u>Georgia</u> Nicolson is Louise Rennison's series for teenage girls, and huge in both Britain and America, where her fans meet to "talk British." The series began with *Angus, Thongs and Full-Frontal Snogging*, and later titles include *On the Bright Side, I'm Now the Girlfriend of a Sex God*; *Dancing in My Nuddy Pants*; and *Knocked Out by My Nunga-Nungas*.

4. LITERARY LASTS

(Appropriately, because it's the last connections question in the book.)

Giles Foden's <u>Last</u> *King of Scotland* (1998) was about Idi Amin, who claimed that title for himself when he was president of Uganda. In the film of the book, Foden had a cameo role as a journalist.

Kazantzakis's <u>Last</u> *Temptation of Christ* (1951) depicted Jesus struggling with fears and doubts— and was soon placed on the Index of Prohibited Books by the Vatican. Martin Scorsese's film version of 1988 caused a similar fuss, especially among born-again Christians. (Kazantzakis's *Zorba the Greek* made for a less controversial film, and launched a thousand package tours instead.)

A10

Uncas is the <u>last</u> of the Mohicans in James Fenimore Cooper's novel of the same name.

Socrates's trial for corrupting the minds of Athenian youth, and his death by being made to drink hemlock, are described in *The <u>Last</u> Days of Socrates* by his pupil, Plato.

Round Five

And Finally: Literary Lasts, Conclusions, and Farewells

1. Christopher Isherwood. *Goodbye to Berlin* and Isherwood's earlier book *Mr. Norris Changes Trains* were the basis of the musical *Cabaret*.

2. Hubert Selby Jr. In 1966, the book was successfully prosecuted in Britain under the Obscene Publications Act, when one of the witnesses for the prosecution was Robert Maxwell. The verdict was overturned two years later in an appeal brought by John Mortimer. (Chapter 2 of *Last Exit to Brooklyn*, by the way, is called "The Queen Is Dead"—which is where the Smiths got the title of their most highly acclaimed album.)

3. Hugh (or H. R.) Trevor-Roper—who did much to unmake his name thirty-six years later when he declared the forged Hitler diaries to be genuine.

4. Robert Browning

5. *The Amber Spyglass*

6. *The Ghost Road*

7. T. C. Boyle

8. "The Rime of the Ancient Mariner" by Samuel Taylor Coleridge

9. Edmund White's

10. "The rest is silence."

A10

1. From "Locksley Hall" by Alfred, Lord Tennyson

2. From *Heart of Darkness* by Joseph Conrad

3. From "An Essay on Criticism" by Alexander Pope

4. From "Meditation XVII" by John Donne

5. From "If" by Rudyard Kipling

6. From "Pippa Passes" by Robert Browning

Acknowledgments and Thanks

The rounds of literary mistakes draw partly on a section in *Flaubert's Parrot* by Julian Barnes, which in turn drew on (and led me to) a lecture by Christopher Ricks.

My warmest thanks to all those involved in *The Write Stuff* over the years, including the endlessly impressive team captains, John Walsh and Sebastian Faulks, who you might be depressed to hear get almost all the questions right; the producers, Jon Rolph, Dawn Ellis, and Katie Marsden; our regular extracts reader, Beth Chalmers; all the guests; and John Pidgeon, Caroline Raphael, and Mark Damazer at Radio 4.

Thanks to Jeanette Shaw at Perigee Books for her help with Americanizing (or, as I'd once have said, Americanising) the original British book—including her many valuable tips on the names of American chocolate bars.

Finally, many thanks as ever to my wife, Helen, who did too much of the work looking after Sam while I was writing all of this—and yet who still found time to make helpful suggestions.

Permissions

(No peeking before doing the quizzes.)

All reasonable efforts have been made by the author and the publisher to trace the copyright holders of the material quoted in the book. In the event that the author or publisher is contacted by any of the untraceable copyright holders after the publication of this book, the author and publisher will endeavor to rectify the position accordingly.

The author and publishers gratefully acknowledge permission granted to reproduce extracts from the following:

1988). Copyright © 1988 by Space Time Publications. Reprinted by permission of RandomHouse Inc.

Hemingway, Ernest. A letter to Scott Fitzgerald (July 1, 1925), *Ernest Hemingway: Selected Letters, 1917–1961*, edited by Carlos Baker (Scribner, 2003). Copyright © 1981 by Hemingway Foreign Rights Trust. Reprinted by permission of Simon & Schuster Inc.

Hornby, Nick. *About a Boy* (Victor Gollancz, 1998). Copyright © 1998 by Nick Hornby. Reproduced by permission of Penguin Group (USA) Inc.

Hosseini, Khaled. *The Kite Runner* (Riverhead, 2003). Copyright © 2003 by Khaled Hosseini. Reproduced by permission of Penguin Group (USA) Inc.

Irving, John. *A Prayer for Owen Meany* (William Morrow, 1989). Copyright © 1989 by John Irving. Reproduced by permission of RandomHouse Inc.

Lawrence, D. H. *Lady Chatterley's Lover* (Penguin, 1960) Copyright © 1960 by the Estate of D. H. Lawrence. Reproduced by permission of Pollinger Limited and the Estate of Frieda Lawrence Ravagli.

Marx, Groucho. Letter from T. S. Eliot, *The Groucho Letters: Letters from and to Groucho Marx* by Groucho Marx (Simon & Schuster, 1967). Copyright © 1967 by Groucho Marx. Reproduced by permission of Simon & Schuster Inc.

McEwan, Ian. *On Chesil Beach* (Bantam Dell, 2007). Copyright, © 2007 by Ian McEwan. Reprinted by permission of RandomHouse Inc.

Miller, Arthur. *Timebends: A Life* (Grove Press, 1989). Copyright © 1987 by Arthur Miller. Reproduced by permission of Grove/Atlantic Inc.

Moore, Michael. *Stupid White Men* (Harper Perennial,

2001). Copyright © 2001 by Michael Moore. Reproduced by permission of HarperCollins, Inc.

Nabokov, Vladimir. *Lolita* (Penguin, 1959). Copyright © 1955 by Vladimir Nabokov. Reproduced by permission of Penguin Group (USA) Inc.

Oshinsky, David. Knopf's reader's report on *The Diary of Anne Frank*, from "No Thanks, Mr. Nabokov," *New York Times Sunday Book Review*, September 9, 2007. Copyright © 2007 by *The New York Times*. Reproduced by permission of *The New York Times*.

Proust, Marcel. *The Remembrance of Things Past*, translated C. K. Scott Moncrieff and Terence Kilmartin (Penguin, 1954). Translation copyright © 1981 by Chatto & Windus and RandomHouse Inc. Reprinted by permission of Penguin Group (USA) Inc.

Roth, Philip. *The Human Stain* (Houghton Mifflin Harcourt, 2000). Copyright © 2000 by Philip Roth. Reproduced by permission of Houghton Mifflin Harcourt.

Shaw, George Bernard. Speech at Moscow's Trade Union Central Hall, *Bernard Shaw: The Definitive One-Volume Edition* by Michael Holroyd (W. W. Norton, 1995). Copyright © 1997 by Michael Holroyd. Reproduced by permission of the Society of Authors, on behalf of the Bernard Shaw Estate.

Smith, Dodie. *The Hundred and One Dalmatians* (Viking, 1956). Copyright © 1956 by the Estate of Dodie Smith. Reprinted by permission of Penguin Group (USA) Inc.

Spark, Muriel. *The Prime of Miss Jean Brodie* (J. B. Lippincott, 1962). Copyright © 1961 by Muriel Spark. Reproduced by permission of David Higham Associates Limited.

Tolstoy, Leo. *Anna Karenina,* translated by Rosemary Edmonds (Penguin Classics, 1954). Translation copyright © 1954 by Rosemary Edmonds. Reproduced by permission of Penguin Group (USA) Inc.

Tolstoy, Leo. *War and Peace*, translated by Constance Garnett (Penguin, 1904). Translation copyright © 1904 by Constance Garnett. Reproduced by permission of Penguin Group (USA) Inc.

Updike, John. *Memories of the Ford Administration* (Knopf, 1992). Copyright © 1992 John Updike. Reproduced by permission of RandomHouse Inc.

Wodehouse, P. G. "Rodney Has a Relapse," *Nothing Serious* (Herbert Jenkins, 1950). Copyright © 1950 by the Trustees of the Wodehouse Estate Rogers. Reproduced by permission of Rogers, Coleridge & White Ltd.

Wolfe, Tom. *The Bonfire of the Vanities* (Farrar Straus Giroux, 1987). Copyright © 1987 by Tom Wolfe. Reprinted by permission of Farrar Straus Giroux.

Woolf, Virginia. *The Diary of Virginia Woolf*, vol. 2 (Hogarth Press). Used by permission of the executors of the Virginia Woolf Estate and Harcourt Brace.